SPIRITUAL
DISCERNMENT

Writings by Joel S. Goldsmith

A Message for the Ages

A Parenthesis in Eternity

Awakening Mystical Consciousness

Beyond Words and Thoughts

Collected Essays

Conscious Union with God

Consciousness in Transition

Consciousness Is What I Am

Consciousness Transformed

Consciousness Unfolding

God Formed Us for His Glory

God, the Substance of All Form

I Stand on Holy Ground

Invisible Supply

Leave Your Nets

Living Between Two Worlds

Living by Grace

Living by the Word

Living Now

Living the Illumined Life

Living the Infinite Way

Man Was Not Born to Cry

Our Spiritual Resources

Practicing the Presence

Realization of Oneness

Rising in Consciousness

Seek Ye First

Showing Forth the Presence of God

Spiritual Discernment

Spiritual Interpretation of Scripture

Spiritual Power of Truth

The Altitude of Prayer

The Art of Meditation

The Art of Spiritual Healing

The Art of Spiritual Living

The Christmas Letters

The Contemplative Life

The Early Years

The Easter Letters

The Foundation of Mysticism

The Gift of Love

The Heart of Mysticism: Vols. I–VI

The Infinite Way

The Joel Goldsmith Reader

The Journey Back to the Father's House

The Master Speaks

The Mystical I

The Only Freedom

The Thunder of Silence

The World Is New

All titles listed above can be found at www.AcropolisBooks.com.

SPIRITUAL
DISCERNMENT
THE HEALING CONSCIOUSNESS

Joel S. Goldsmith

Edited by
Lorraine Sinkler

Acropolis Books, Publisher
Longboat Key, Florida

SPIRITUAL DISCERNMENT

Copyright © 1973-1974 by Emma A. Goldsmith
Copyright © 1977, 2002 by Thelma G. McDonald

For information contact:
Acropolis Books, Inc.
Longboat Key, Florida
http://www.acropolisbooks.com

Book design by Palomar Print Design

Library of Congress Cataloging-in-Publication Data

Goldsmith, Joel S., 1892–1964.
Spiritual discernment : the healing consciousness / Joel S. Goldsmith; edited
by Lorraine Sinkler.
    p. cm.
Includes bibliographical references and index.
ISBN 978-1-889051-63-5
1. Spiritual life. 2. Discernment (Christian theology) 3. Spiritual healing.
4. New Thought. I. Sinkler, Lorraine. II. Title.

BF639.G56886 2003
299'.93--dc21   2002155974

Except the Lord build the house,
they labour in vain that build it.

Psalm 127

"Illumination dissolves all material ties and binds men together with the golden chains of spiritual understanding; it acknowledges only the leadership of the Christ; it has no ritual or rule but the divine, impersonal universal Love; no other worship than the inner Flame that is ever lit at the shrine of Spirit. This union is the free state of spiritual brotherhood. The only restraint is the discipline of Soul; therefore, we know liberty without license; we are a united universe without physical limits; a divine service to God without ceremony or creed. The illumined walk without fear—by Grace."

From *The Infinite Way* by Joel S. Goldsmith

DEDICATION

TWENTIETH CENTURY MYSTIC Joel S. Goldsmith revealed to the Western world the nature and substance of mystical living that demonstrated how mankind can live in the consciousness of God. The clarity and insight of his teachings, called The Infinite Way, were captured in more than thirty-five books and in over twelve hundred hours of tape recordings that, today, perpetuate his message.

Joel faithfully arranged to have prepared from his class tapes, monthly letters which were made available as one of the most important tools to assist students in their study and application of The Infinite Way teachings. He felt each of these letters came from an ever-new insight that would produce a deeper level of understanding and awareness of truth as students worked diligently with this fresh and timely material.

Each yearly compilation of the *Letters* focused on a central theme, and it became apparent that working with an entire year's material built an ascending level of consciousness. The *Letters* were subsequently published as books, each containing all the year's letters. The publications became immensely popular as they proved to be of great assistance in the individual student's development of spiritual awareness.

Starting in 1954, the monthly letters were made available to students wishing to subscribe to them. Each year of the *Letters* was published individually during 1954 through 1959 and made available in book form. From 1960 through

1970 the *Letters* were published and renamed as books with the titles:

1960 Letters	*Our Spiritual Resources*
1961 Letters	*The Contemplative Life*
1962 Letters	*Man Was Not Born to Cry*
1963 Letters	*Living Now*
1964 Letters	*Realization of Oneness*
1965 Letters	*Beyond Words and Thoughts*
1966 Letters	*The Mystical I*
1967 Letters	*Living Between Two Worlds*
1968 Letters	*The Altitude of Prayer*
1969 Letters	*Consciousness Is What I Am*
1970 Letters	*Awakening Mystical Consciousness*

Joel worked closely with his editor, Lorraine Sinkler, to ensure each letter carried the continuity, integrity, and pure consciousness of the message. After Joel's transition in 1964, Emma A. Goldsmith (Joel's wife) requested that Lorraine continue working with the monthly letters, drawing as in the past from the inexhaustible tape recordings of his class work with students. The invaluable work by Lorraine and Emma has ensured that this message will be preserved and available in written form for future generations. Acropolis Books is honored and privileged to offer in book form the next eleven years of Joel's teaching.

The 1971 through 1981 *Letters* also carry a central theme for each year, and have been renamed with the following titles:

1971 Letters	*Living by the Word*
1972 Letters	*Living the Illumined Life*
1973 Letters	*Seek Ye First*
1974 Letters	*Spiritual Discernment: the Healing Consciousness*
1975 Letters	*A Message for the Ages*
1976 Letters	*I Stand on Holy Ground*
1977 Letters	*The Art of Spiritual Living*
1978 Letters	*God Formed Us for His Glory*
1979 Letters	*The Journey Back to the Father's House*
1980 Letters	*Showing Forth the Presence of God*
1981 Letters	*The Only Freedom*

Acropolis Books dedicates this series of eleven books to Lorraine Sinkler and Emma A. Goldsmith for their ongoing commitment to ensure that these teachings will never be lost to the world.

TABLE OF CONTENTS

Spiritual
Discernment

❖ 1 ❖

PEELING OFF THE ONION SKINS

IN THE HISTORY of the world, it is recorded that those who received the greatest light were those who were in deepest need of spiritual light and who had to search more seriously and diligently than the persons who were getting along comfortably without God.

It takes desperation of one sort or another to drive us deep enough into the heart of God to find God. As a rule, it is only when human companionship has not sufficed, when human supply has not given us enough happiness, satisfaction, or completeness, and when even human health has not made us relax in an inner peace that we ask, "Lord, Lord, where art Thou?"

Then it is that we begin the search for truth. Then it is that we try to find out if there is not a God, if there is not a Something somewhere that would bring to us what we are seeking. And what are we seeking? Most of all, peace. If we had peace, we would not be disturbed by physical, mental, or financial discomfort. But we have not found peace. We think that we can find peace if we have enough education, a good job, or a happy marriage, but even if we do enjoy financial comfort, good family relationships, and all other desirable human things, very often there is still something else that we have not achieved, and out of that hunger comes the search.

As far as Joel Goldsmith was concerned, he was a businessman, and he was not doing too badly in the business world except for some momentary periods that everyone sooner or later has in business. There was no idea in his mind that he would at any time ever be connected with a religious, philosophical, or metaphysical work. That was no part of his consciousness. At best, it can be said that he had that hunger to find something more satisfying than a highball, a game of cards, a theater, a dance, or even a successful business, and that he was trying to find something better than those things.

Most of us come to the grace of God through our ills and our discords. I was very ill, nothing more serious, however, than a severe nasty cold, one of those bad Great Lakes winter colds. I could not rise above it and so I looked up a practitioner and found a man of whom I had never heard before who told me he did not take patients on Saturday because he devoted that day to study and prayer, but who, when he saw the condition I was in, invited me into his office. I not only had an instantaneous healing, but when I went out of his office I could not smoke any more; I could not drink any more; and I could not play cards any more. Two days later someone asked me for a healing and received it. The day after that someone else came to me and said, "Would you pray for me?" and she had a healing. That kept up for a year and a half, and by that time I was in the practice of healing.

I had no idea of entering into the practice of spiritual healing: it just came upon me. I was in the healing work sixteen years, and during that time a whole series of unfoldments and experiences came to me that resulted in the publication of the book, *The Infinite Way*. One step after another led to a worldwide healing and teaching ministry, but never once was there the idea of going into such an activity.

Being Unselfed Ensures Success

Success can come only when there is no individual desiring success, no one desiring to save the world, to heal or teach the world. When there is an individual who has caught a glimpse of truth or, by the grace of God, has been given a little healing or teaching gift, and when that individual is willing to share it without any thought of saving anybody, including himself, or supplying anybody, including himself, out of that comes a thriving and successful activity.

An activity of God operates in human consciousness and, if we are sufficiently willing, It operates through us and makes us go out and do Its work. We do not plan it that way. It operates, It goes through our consciousness and then calls us to do Its work.

I tell you all this to bring to light a secret that will ensure success in any activity in which you may be engaged, and the success will come because of the activity of truth in your consciousness. You will not have to advertise; you will not have to tell anybody that you are following a spiritual path, or that you believe in God. You will never have to open your lips of your own accord, because this principle absolutely sets aside any sense of self that might interfere with your demonstration and permits it to be a demonstration of God.

Deglorifying the Personal Sense of Self

In spiritual or mystical writings, it is always taught that the spiritual aspirant must get rid of the self, with a small "s," or put aside the self. The little self must grow smaller so that the big Self can become greater in individual experience.

Here is a principle found in the teaching of the Master Christ Jesus which will guarantee the destruction of your self and assure the rebirth of your real Self, of the *I* that you are. The teaching is that there are two things that you must not do in public: you must not pray where men can see you, and you must not do your alms or benevolences where men can see you. Think what it would mean if you were to set aside something of your income for a spiritual purpose, and if nobody were to know about it or to know where it went, or even to suspect you were benevolent or charitable. As far as the rest of the world was concerned it might even think, because you would never mention such things, that you did not give to charity, benevolences, community funds, or a spiritual activity.

Think what it would mean if nobody ever knew that you prayed. That was such a secret from the world that the world probably thought you were slightly atheistic because it never heard you speak of praying and never saw you pray. Think how your little self would be deglorified and deflated.

On the other hand, think how you would glorify your self if, judging by the Bibles you carry around or the fact that you haven't missed church attendance in twenty-seven years, six months, and four weeks, the world could point to you and say how generous you are or how holy you are. That inflates the self; it gives glory to you, but in that degree it cheats you of the God-experience. Did not the Master reveal that those things that the Father sees in secret He rewards openly?

So when you are not seeking praise because of your charitableness or because of your mercifulness or benevo-lence, you are deflating your self, and you are permitting the *I* that you are to perform Its work, and because It operates in the invisible, the presence and power of God in the invisible appear visibly and tangibly in the world.

Intellectual Agreement May
Precede Spiritual Awareness

When you turn to a spiritual study, you are beginning to realize your oneness with God even though at first you do it only intellectually. Even though intellectually you agree that you are to "call no man your father upon the earth; for one is your Father, which is in heaven,"[1] neither you nor I can realize the spiritual import of that when it is first heard or read. But if you are a sincere student, something within you will say, "Yes, that really must be the truth. Only God can make a tree, and so I am willing to agree that only God made me and that God must be the creative principle of my being." Agreeing with that is not going to do anything special for you. You have taken only the first step, intellectually agreeing that God is the creative principle of your being.

Later on you read, "Son, thou art ever with me, and all that I have is thine."[2] That truth may be more difficult to agree with because appearances may not testify to it. It does not look at all as if you have all that God has. But as you continue in your study and if you are patient, you will realize in contemplating the nature of God that God is life and that the life which is God is your life. Then you discover that God is the intelligence of the universe, and any intelligence you have is the intelligence of God. Soon you will be agreeing with the statement, "Son, ... all that I have is thine," and you will know that all the Father has is yours. You will not be able to demonstrate it yet because up to this point you have probably only agreed with it intellectually. In fact, probably you say, "Yes, now I can see that it is true, but so what?"

You go from one truth to another and, if you are at all like most persons, you will someday say to yourself, "Well, I know all the truth that is to be known, but it doesn't seem to do much for me. I saw so-and-so get a healing. I wonder why it doesn't work for me." The answer is that so far it has been only an intellectual acceptance of the truth: it has not been the spiritual discernment of it. It has not been an inner conviction; it has not come with spiritual power to make itself alive.

It is for that reason that students have to study and practice for years. It is like peeling off onion skins. When you first come to a spiritual study, you are as thick as a big onion and as opaque. As you continue to study and catch a little glimpse here and a little glimpse there, an onion skin of grossness and of materiality drops away. It is not enough to notice. You look at yourself and feel that you are making no progress whatsoever. Maybe a few months later, another onion skin drops off, and you look in the mirror and say, "I am just as material; I am just as sick; I am just as poor; I am making no progress," and you wonder why you are sticking to your study. You don't really know. You just can't give it up.

Bit by bit one onion skin after another drops away until one day the first realization comes and suddenly you say, "Oh, I see." And what do you see? "Oh, I don't know, I can't explain it to you." That is wisdom because if you could explain it, it would mean that you did not have it. You can never explain spiritual wisdom. Nobody can ever explain spiritual wisdom. All a person can do is reveal in human intellectual terms what happens in his consciousness.

The Spiritual Perception
of a Principle Is Necessary

When the principle of secrecy was revealed to me—of not praying in public and of not giving alms in public—that was an inner spiritual experience. But when I give that revelation to you, it is not a spiritual experience to you. It is merely the statement of a principle which you intellectually accept or reject. If you live with it long enough, however, you will know it so thoroughly that you will never again be tempted to make a display either of your religious convictions or your charities. If someone asks you about them, you will not be able to answer him except to refer to the passages of the Master in the Gospels, but you will not be able to tell him what you feel any more than I can tell you.

There are many spiritual principles other than secrecy found in the Bible and expounded and expanded in Infinite Way writings, but even though you have a feeling within you that all this is true, do not expect any miracles from that. The miracles do not occur until you begin to catch the spiritual perception of the principle, the inner "click," the inner awareness, the inner light. Students who have been studying for years and feel they have not made the progress they should have made should not judge by appearances because they may be next door to their spiritual demonstration. No one knows how close he is to spiritual realization because it is true of every one of us that we are humanly opaque even the very minute before spiritual illumination comes.

When You Think Not

Illumination always seems to come in a blinding flash, but it has been coming gradually without your knowledge from the minute that you turned to a spiritual teaching. The very minute you turned to anything of a transcendental nature, you started a little stir under those onion skins, and you were preparing the way for them to begin breaking away from the core that held them together. Then "in such an hour as ye think not,"[3] one of them drops off—but you are not aware of its dropping away. Who is going to miss one onion skin off a whole onion! You may have to come all the way down to three-quarters of that onion dropping away before you look in the mirror and say, "How slender I am! What has happened to me? That can't be I." No, it can't be you, but it is *I:* it is the one *I* showing through. The opaqueness is somewhat dissolved; there is more of a transparency there; and you can begin to see through to the center.

So on a Saturday, the wrong day of the week, the practitioner to whom I had turned for help wasn't going to see anybody. He was going to get the truth all for himself on Saturday and show it forth on Monday. But I didn't have until Monday, and so on that Saturday, convinced within myself that I had made no progress and that I wasn't any further advanced in the spiritual awareness than I had been thirteen years before, on that day of all days enough light broke through so I could do healing work, and after thirteen years of study many human traits fell away from me in that one day. All that time, however, without my knowing it or being aware of it, onion skins had been falling away, but in that one day the realization came.

Motive Is All-Important

Saul of Tarsus had spent years and years and years studying about God and praying, and to our sense it would seem that he was not going about it in the right way. The proof that there was not anything wrong about what he was doing was that in one blinding flash the full light was given to him. So we must recognize that the Hebrew way is right, the Protestant way, the Catholic way, the Hindu way, the Mohammedan way—any way is right *if* the desire is to know God.

When you are willing to sacrifice your life, your money, your time, and your effort for your concept of God, someday you will lose that concept of God and find the one true God. That is what happened to Saul. In a blinding flash, he lost the traditional Hebrew concept of God and gained the vision and the experience of God which is far better than any concept. A concept is only a concept, never God, and when you have the experience of God Itself, you will know how foolish you were to believe that your concepts were correct. Each one of you in turn will someday come face to face with the God-experience as Saul did, but only when you have risen above the letter of truth into the spirit or consciousness of truth.

It is never true when you say, "I Am That I Am,"[4] or, "Before Abraham was, I am,"[5] and say it only intellectually, because you are speaking of yourself as a human being. The moment that transitional experience takes place which reveals spiritual life, however, and you say, "Oh, that *I* is eternal. I am that I," you have joined the group of mystics. You have joined with Moses, with Jesus, and with all those who realize the true nature of that invisible Selfhood which does not glorify Itself in the outer realm but is glorified only by the effect of Itself. That *I* which we realize in secret now shows Itself forth in better health, more ample supply, greater peace of mind, and happier human relationships, although not necessarily in what the world calls happiness. Do not look for that. You will not find it. That is a state of deadness.

But there is a state of mind which is at peace regardless of the outer circumstances or conditions of life. Jesus could be nailed to the cross, but do not think for a moment that he lost his peace or that he thought he was losing his life. In the attainment of the inner spiritual vision, he could give up his body and then pick it up again. Do not think for a minute that if God is life eternal, anyone can destroy that life. If God is infinite life, your life and mine, it will never be destroyed. Your agreeing intellectually with this will not do the works for you, but by abiding in it, eventually you will pass from the letter of truth to the actual experience or demonstration of the spiritual discernment of truth.

Perseverance Requisite

At this moment you may be agreeing only intellectually that these things are true and feel that you cannot prove them or show them forth. In fact, you cannot even feel them. Everyone has gone through that phase, and not only for a year: some have gone through it two, three, seven, or eight years, and there are reasons to believe that there are persons who have gone through it for thirty years. You think, "What! The possibility of looking forward to that!" Yes, there is that possibility, and you might as well be prepared for it and say, "I have to keep going on because where would I go if I stopped? I have nothing to go back to, so even if it does take thirty or forty years I might as well stay on the path until the light breaks through."

If you stick to the correct letter of truth, you will attain spiritual wisdom and, if your motive and desire for God are as pure as those of Saul of Tarsus, you will arrive. This does not mean that the correct letter of truth alone is going to take you into heaven. While it is good not to be filled with some of the errors that exist in many teachings, there is enough light in any teaching of integrity for a person who is not completely sectarian in his outlook to lead him to the kingdom, if he has the attitude, "I don't care what you call me. My motive is to find God. My desire is to find God, not to glorify Protestantism, Catholicism, Divine Science, Christian Science, Unity, or The Infinite Way. I don't care about them. What I care about is my relationship to God and the attainment of it." If you are following any spiritual or religious teaching and not thinking of it as some kind of a glorified something or other, but merely as a means to bring you to the light of revelation, then any of them will suffice.

That will not be true if you take a teaching and look on it as something infallible whose rules and regulations you must follow. If you are to benefit from a teaching, you should look on it as a step, as a help, or as an aid toward your realization of God, and then you will attain it. You will. There is enough truth in any one of them to lead you right to the kingdom of God if your motive is to achieve the realization of God.

You can find God through the study of the letter of truth combined with meditation, prayer, and a very humble desire to know God. But you will not gain eternal life merely by following a religious teaching. You will gain eternal life only by knowing God aright. There have been Catholic and Protestant mystics who knew God—Christian Science, Unity, New Thought, and Infinite Way students. All you have to do is to be concerned with your goal of knowing God and then stay with it through the trials and tribulations that come until those onion skins fall off, enough of them to bring you to the spiritual experience of knowing God.

Beware of a Messianic Complex

When that experience takes place, you will lose all anxiety, all concern, and all fear for yourself. Sick or well, alive or dead, you are just the same infinite spiritual being that you are now, and so you will not be too concerned whether you are a little sick or a little well, a little dead or a little alive. Whether you live in one state or another or whether you live on one plane of consciousness or another will not disturb you. Fear drops away; false responsibility drops away; and then instead of having to support yourself purely by physical or mental means, your support begins to flow without taking anxious thought for your life. Instead of establishing health by the process of thought-taking and knowing the truth, your health is taken care of as if there really were a God who cared, because by this time you have come into the actual experience of God caring.

At this point two things may happen, and you have to watch yourself and not let them happen—at least not let them get too great a hold on you. One is that you begin to be concerned about members of your family who do not know this truth, and you want to drag them right into heaven with you. Get over that quickly, or they may drag you down to their level. You might as well let them work out their own salvation, and if they are to come up they will come up through Grace or through difficulties the same as you did. But trying to save them their difficulties and trying to take them up the easy way, it is more likely that they will take you down than that you will take them up.

The second concern is that you want to give what has been given you to the world. Somebody writes to me, "Oh, come over to England. They need this." Somebody else writes "Oh, come to Africa. They need this." And I say, "Brother, if there is any spot on the globe that needs it more than the United States of America and more specifically Washington, D.C., I would like to hear about it."

It is needed in all these places. But there is one place where it is needed even more—in me. I need it even more than they do. So do you. You would be surprised how much we need it, because no matter how much we have seen of the truth we have only glimpsed it. There isn't anyone here or anybody on earth who has more than glimpsed it. It is true that some are showing it forth in greater degree than others, aware of it to a greater degree.

Since I have been in this work, I have had the privilege of meeting quite a few mystics, illumined souls. Always they are regretful and sorry that they have so little to offer because they have only glimpsed a little. And it is not false modesty; it is true. In comparison with what God is, we have caught only the possibilities, the potentiality of the vision.

Do not get all puffed up with the idea that as a person, you have something with which to save the world because you have not. Nobody of himself is going to save the world. It has been my experience that I cannot save even one individual, and I can truthfully say in twenty-five years of my work I do not know of one single soul that I have saved, not one.

Through this unfoldment of God as individual being, I have seen some persons come to their own realization and demonstration of God, but they did it: they were longing for it; they were looking for it. They were opening themselves to the Christ-activity and then with a little glimpse that pops out from me once in a while, they are helped. But I did not do it: they did.

We cannot save the world; we cannot save an individual. All that we can do is to bring about our own delivery from bondage to human sense. Then when we have achieved it, those who are open and receptive and responsive can come and receive a bit of the light that is shining through us.

They themselves must claim it for their own and demonstrate it. So do not permit yourself to get the idea that now you have this light, you are going out to save the world, your relatives, or your friends. Keep your spiritual light secret. Keep it sacred. If others discern it, share it with them to the extent of their capacity to receive it. Silently and sacredly, let that light flow through you to the world, but keep it secret; keep it sacred.

Since this work began, I have never gone any place until I was sent for. I have never gone any place until I was invited. In most of the cases I have had many invitations before I even went once. I am not trying to save the world. I am not going anywhere to carry the gospel. It is not my function to save you; it is not my function to convert you to God; it is not my function to mind your business. It is my function to mind my business, to go away for forty days or four hundred days and live my communion with God and then if by chance you say, "Give me some of that meat. Give me some of that drink, that wine, that water. Give me some of that spiritual food," I respond to that call and share the light with you insofar as I have received it.

The Grace of God Is the Sufficiency unto Every Call

You have to work with it, even if at first it is on the intellectual plane, until the time comes when it passes transitionally from an intellectual agreement to a spiritual experience. Then when your spiritual experience comes, it will not be long before you are called upon for healings, for instruction, or for guidance, and since the call is made upon you, God's grace must give you the wisdom and the healing power to answer it. When a call is made upon you, you must understand that God's grace is your sufficiency and then respond. Whatever call is made upon you, you will be able to respond to it. There will be nothing greater than your capacity because it will be

God-capacity. The deeper things will still go to those more qualified through their greater awareness. The more a person has the more will be expected of him.

When you are called upon to heal or to teach, if you will realize immediately that you do not know enough for that, but the grace of God that gave you the call will give you the answer, you will perform it well. If you make the mistake of believing that you have a good understanding or enough understanding to begin to teach, however, you will make shipwreck of your experience because you never will have enough understanding to heal or to teach.

As you continuously realize, not with false modesty, but with a clear understanding that whatever spiritual grace you have is the grace of God, you can never fail to heal and to teach, and you can lead those who come to you to truth only through the realization that the grace of God that brought the call to you is the grace of God that answers the call. As you sit quietly in the silence, God will speak in some unmistakable way, not necessarily in words or thoughts, but the activity of God will make Itself evident and the results will follow.

At many times you may have tried to heal and not succeeded even though you knew the truth. It was because at that time it was only an intellectual knowledge of truth, and that will not work because the intellectual knowledge of truth is but a stepping stone, one of the means by which we achieve the spiritual realization of it.

Attain a conscious communion with God. Attain the ability to throw your whole dependence on the Infinite Invisible instead of on some person or circumstance in the outer. If you have no object or thought in your mind of using it for a public ministry or to be a practitioner, then step by step you will be led to the experience of God. After that you can retire into the country and never be seen of men again, living your communion with God and doing whatever work you do for the world on the inner plane, or you can go out into the public ministry. The important thing is that you attain the God-experience.

ACROSS THE DESK

So many students have written requesting the titles of the recordings from which the letter is taken each month that I have asked Lorraine, our editor, to indicate the source. You will notice that the titles of the tapes used are given at the [back of the book.] We trust that this information will be of interest to all students who recognize the importance of the letter as the central core of their study for the month and who work with it daily.

Nineteen hundred seventy-three has seen our nation and the world faced with challenging problems of almost insurmountable difficulty. Many of you, too, face challenges of similar seriousness. In the midst of these difficulties, let us give thanks and bear witness to the omnipresent Grace which in Its all-encompassing wisdom is the answer to every problem. Enter into the beginning of this new calendar year with joy and thanksgiving because you know that God is and that God is forever functioning. Underneath, a divine activity is in operation.

TAPE RECORDED EXCERPTS
Prepared by the Editor

The New Year is a time for taking stock and for re-evaluation. The basic question is: Are we going to live under the law of as-ye-sow-so-shall-ye-reap or will we rise out of the law into a life by Grace?

Sowing and Reaping

"What is the sowing and the reaping that is causing the distresses of the people on earth? Paul summed it up. ... 'For he that soweth to the flesh shall of the flesh reap corruption; but he that soweth to the Spirit shall of the Spirit reap life everlasting.' That is the statement, and the explanation is this: you were born into a material sense of life; therefore, you have been sowing to the flesh all your human life. You have put your entire hope, faith, and confidence in form or effect."

Joel S. Goldsmith, "Transcendental Consciousness,"
The 1963 Kailua Private Class.

"'For he that soweth to his flesh, shall of the flesh reap corruption' means literally that as you follow a materialistic state of consciousness, you will reap materiality, not necessarily bad materiality. It can be good materiality, but it will be materiality. It will not be spirituality. ... When you sow to the Spirit, that is quite a different thing. Then it does not say that you will reap good. It says that you will 'reap life everlasting'—eternality or immortality. ...

"Make the acknowledgment that karmic law operates in the experience of every human being. Every human being is under the law of cause and effect. ... As the world comes to us for help, it is a simple matter to recognize that the law of cause and effect is operating. Whatever the ill or discord, it is the result of a universal karmic law. ..."

Joel S. Goldsmith,
"Old Testament: the Law; New Testament: Grace and Truth,"
The 1956 First Steinway Hall Practitioner Class.

❉ 2 ❉

God Must Be an Experience, Not a Concept

It is evident that whatever people have leaned or depended upon, whether material or mental, has not met their needs, and now the desperateness of the world situation is turning their attention to God. Many may seek in wrong directions, but in the end this will be of no major importance since it is not so much the way a person goes that counts, but the motive that impels him. Regardless of what path he chooses, be it ever so false, it will lead him to the kingdom of God if the motive behind his search is a true motive. If the motive that governs his life is a deep desire for truth or for God, he will find himself illumined and actually receiving the gift of the Christ Itself.

In this age, however, students devote far too much attention to the demonstration of the joys and successes that are to come with illumination than they do to the illumination itself. Most truth-students are seeking the demonstration of forms of good, rather than the unfoldment of good.

It is natural, normal, and right that we come into the realization and demonstration of spiritual harmony. But what determines the degree of our success is whether our motive is to leave our "nets"[1] or to have our nets filled with fish. Every person can easily determine the integrity of his motive for himself. The continuous desire to increase the human sense of supply, the human sense of health, or the human sense of success is really an attempt to fill our nets with more fish, larger fish, or tastier fish; whereas the spiritual motive is to leave our nets and find the meaning of "My kingdom."

Beyond Words to the Word

There is a deep spiritual significance in the word *My:* "My kingdom is not of this world.[2]... My peace I give unto you.[3]... My word... shall not return unto me void.[4]... My thoughts are not your thoughts."[5] *My* word, the word of power, is not your word or my word: it is nothing that you or I think, nothing that we have heard from another. *My* word is a word that we can hear only in the inner ear. We can never hear it from a person or read it in a book. We can receive it only within our consciousness from the depths of our being.

When we do hear it, we find it literally true that "the word of God is quick, and powerful, and sharper than any two-edged sword,"[6] that it really does go to the very marrow of the bone and that it divides the Red Sea. No thought that we think and no statement of truth that we know will do that. It is always a truth that is received in consciousness from the depths of our own being.

In The Infinite Way we must go beyond the realm of mind to that realm which is the Source or Spirit. There we receive light and the Word. Many words of The Infinite Way message have been printed, and many, many more have been recorded on tape, but all of these have but one purpose: to drive us back into that kingdom within our own being, to drive us to that level of consciousness where Truth imparts Itself to us. Every word that has been spoken or written in this message has had but one intent: to lift consciousness into an atmosphere where we may individually receive the impartation of Truth.

*Individual Identity
Lost in the Prodigal-State*

In spiritual illumination we discover the great truth that God is infinite, omnipresent, and omnipotent. We learn that God is law, in fact the only law unto all existence, the substance and the activity of all that is. When a student realizes that, sometimes he mounts onto cloud nine and tries to live out from the God-is-all state of consciousness which has not yet been attained. He forgets that that Allness does not wipe out his individual existence, nor does it eliminate individual identity.

To attempt to eliminate individual identity would be like saying that the ministry of Jesus Christ was a mistake because he not only felt that he, personally and individually, had received a message and a mission from the Father, but that his purpose on earth was to exemplify the message and the mission. He felt a call to heal the sick, raise the dead, and teach and preach the gospel to the poor, because he recognized that there exists what is called human existence, sometimes very good, sometimes very bad.

> For I was an hungred, and ye gave me meat: I was thirsty, and ye gave me drink: I was a stranger, and ye took me in: Naked, and ye clothed me: I was sick, and ye visited me: I was in prison, and ye came unto me.
>
> Matthew 25:35,36

He gave recognition to the fact that there is a state of existence from which we must be awakened or into which must come spiritual illumination.

In the infinity of Its being, God encompasses nothing of a mortal or material nature. Nevertheless, there exists what is called the prodigal experience, a sense of selfhood that has wandered from the Father's house, has set up a separate identity called Joel, Bill, or Mary, and which then has a great deal of trouble caring for that identity. Having set up this selfhood, it now has to support itself, feed itself, find ways and means of clothing and housing itself, and of maintaining its own health and life. This separate identity is of great concern to the person who accepts a false sense of his identity.

Re-establishing God
As Individual Identity

At some period or other, every individual decides that the banquet table is not quite as good as the one that the Father's servant has, and he starts the return to divine consciousness. That is the first step on the path of spiritual realization, leading to illumination. If at that point a person can keep his thought away from demonstrating food and rent, but maintain the hunger and thirst for the Father's house, divine consciousness, the realization of spiritual truth, then comes the transition into that state of consciousness when the Father-consciousness of divine sonship becomes apparent and It again takes over.

The individual returns to his rightful estate of being a beholder of God revealing Itself, God living Its own life, not wiping out the individual but God living Its life in infinite form, infinite variety, God appearing not only as Himself, but God appearing as infinite persons, infinite varieties of flowers, fruit, sun, moon, or stars. The realization of God will not wipe out the sun, moon, stars, fish, plants, or planets, but rather spiritual illumination will reveal God as the individual identity of persons, things, and conditions.

Some students have the impression that they can eliminate themselves merely by saying that since God is all, everybody is in heaven, which is an attempt to wipe out through human words the world of unreality and with it individual identity, instead of wiping it out through right identification. But infinite individuality is a corollary of infinite God. God could no more reveal Itself as a nonentity than It could reveal Itself as just one man or one woman. The infinite nature of God's being must inevitably reveal Itself in infinite forms of expression, in infinite variety, and in infinite individuality. These infinite forms never merge. A potato never becomes an orchid, nor is there such a thing as a potato or an orchid being wiped out and nothing left but blank space, which would be the case if our individualities were erased. There would be nothing then but a oneness that would be a limited sense of One, not an infinite sense of One.

God, infinite, indivisible Being, must express Itself as individual being. It cannot create something other than Itself. It must evolve—not create, but evolve. Out of Its infinity, It must express so that the life which is God is the life of individual being, your being and mine. That mind which is God must be the mind of individual being. We are infinite, not because of any infinity of our own: we are infinite because there is but one Infinity, universally expressing Itself, and in that universality It expresses Itself as your being and mine. Let us glory in the truth of God appearing as infinite individuality, God appearing as the life and substance of our being.

Bearing Witness to
Divine Sonship in Daily Life

There is much of the relative in all teachings, and that inevitably must be because we are using the activity of the mind in order to lift ourselves above the very thoughts and fears of the human mind. Even in spiritual being there is a faculty of awareness known as the human mind which has a legitimate place in our lives. It is not a creative faculty; it is not something used with which to create or change things or conditions; but it is used to become aware of that which is. The human mind may know that two times two is four, but it cannot make it so. The human mind is an instrument through which we learn that there is a law of like begetting like, but the human mind cannot make it so.

As long as it is necessary for us to be aware, there must be a faculty of awareness. As long as there is a need for eating and drinking, there must be those activities called digestion, assimilation, and elimination. What these are in spiritual being and body or how they will appear to us, most persons do not now know. But we do know that the greater our realization of God as the very life of our being, the more harmonious this mind and body appear to us and function for us. We have not risen above the need for a body, and therefore we have not risen above the need for the harmonious functioning of being and body.

In the degree of our conscious oneness with God, our minds and bodies function without any awareness that they are functioning. The blood is flowing; all the organs and functions are operating, and yet not intruding themselves upon our awareness. In the sense and degree of separation from God which is human consciousness, there will be physical, mental, moral, and financial inharmony, and inharmony in human relationships of all kinds. In the degree of conscious union with God, harmony is restored. As spiritual awareness becomes more and more a part of us, we find mind, body, and being operating harmoniously and joyously.

Oftentimes those still under the sense of separation notice the greater harmony in our experience and come to us for help. It is not wise to preach to them, to make light of their problems, to make denials that they have problems or that there is anyone to have a problem. Rather, we should develop our consciousness to the degree that when any person comes to us for help, the light of our being dispels the illusory sense of discord and lifts him into an atmosphere where he, too, realizes his true identity. We do very little talking to anyone who asks for help, very little of preaching, very little of telling him to think better thoughts or to become more loving, just, or moral. Instead, we devote ourselves to rising above even the physical sense of good, living insofar as we can in the spiritual atmosphere of harmony, and then letting the errors of human sense be dispelled by contact with our consciousness. As our lives begin to show forth God's handiwork, the world comes to us for more and more of that experience.

It is important to know the correct letter of truth and to be able to give some measure of reason for our faith. But let us beware lest the thought ever enter our minds that by voicing these truths, writing them, or telling them to a person, we thereby eliminate the discord. The elimination of discords in our experience or in that of those who come to us is the result of the degree of our conscious oneness with God.

As we work through the forms of treatment or contemplative meditation that are given in The Infinite Way writings and recordings, we come step by step to a higher unfoldment. There is a point of transition where every person on the spiritual path passes from living his own life, making his own decisions, and being concerned with his own affairs to a place in consciousness where Something takes over. That

Something has been called by many names. Probably for us the Father within, or Immanuel, God with us, will do.

Affirming, stating, or even thinking that the Christ dwells in us or that the Presence goes before us to lead us by a way we know not will do nothing for us. These statements in and of themselves are not power. The constant remembrance of them, the continuous bringing of them to light within our consciousness will, however, lead us to that point of transition where the Spirit takes over. Then it is no more necessary to make such statements than it would be to walk around saying, "I am honest"; "I am fair"; "I am just"; or "I am moral." The person whose nickname is Honest John immediately arouses a healthy skepticism, and certainly we would also suspect ourselves if we found it necessary to walk around testifying to our honesty or fairness.

So the time must come when it is no longer necessary for us to state or even think, "I am spiritual"; "I am Spirit"; "I am the child of God." Such affirmations automatically drop away when Spirit Itself begins to live our lives. We begin to see that what we have learned is not so much the truth of being as the basis for the *consciousness* of the truth of being.

God Is an Experience, Not a Concept

Everyone has some concept of God, more especially every student of spiritual wisdom. But nobody can reveal what God is since God is Spirit, and the things of the Spirit are foolishness to man. Wherever there have been spiritually minded individuals who have risen to a point of a realized relationship with God, these individuals have had the experience, the knowledge, and the awareness of God, and in their turn have given us their concept of what God is. At best, however, all that they have given is a concept of

God. A concept of God really represents an idea of God, a sense of God, and that concept can be continuously changing. For a while our concept of God may be the Jehovah God of Hebrew scripture, the God of punishment, the God of reward, the God that goes out with armies and destroys other peoples. We may entertain a concept of God that feeds us every day and protects us, but that is not God. That simply represents our concept of God.

The Christian church today has accepted the concept of the Judaic God more than that of the Christian God, that is, the idea of a punishing and rewarding God and of a God of good and evil. All churches to some extent accept the God of the Old Testament.

No concept or definition of God is correct. In fact, there is no way to arrive at a concept of God that is correct. Yet God may define Itself to us within our own consciousness so that we, too, may say with the prophets, "Yet in my flesh shall I see God"[7] or, like Abraham, we may converse and commune with the Father, and have as close a relationship with Him as the Master who had intimate communion with the Father within. But there is no way in which we can define God to another.

God is an experience; God is a realization. When we say that God is mind, God is life, or God is love, we cannot take words like life, mind, love, principle, soul, or spirit and use them as if they were synonyms for God. A synonym is a word that may take the place of another. But words like spirit, soul, mind, or principle are merely descriptive of certain aspects, phases, or facets of God-being. To say that God is mind is to recognize God as the source, fount, and avenue of intelligence. That does make God mind, but it does not make mind God.

In the New Testament God is spoken of as Father, and we entertain that concept of God and surround it with certain meaning. There are persons who think of God as love, and then of all the humanly loving things they can ascribe to God, not realizing that love in John's sense had a much higher connotation than anything that we can humanly understand. Love includes within itself care, protection, and gentleness, but love is not God because there is more to God than love. If we were to take God as the sum total of all the synonyms for God, we still would not realize the infinite nature of God's being. As we progress from the Old Testament to the New, from the New Testament into metaphysics, and from metaphysics to spiritual wisdom, our concepts of God will change, just as our concepts of prayer will change.

Each one of us must have some kind of a God-experience in which God actually takes over and becomes the dominating influence in our lives. Then to the God we have experienced, we give a name. In the days of my own unfoldment on the nature of God, when I could not visualize God as Father or Mother, the Christ became the reality to me. I could understand the word "Christ" as well as I could understand the word "water." I knew what It meant; I felt It; I lived with It; It lived with me; and then along with It came a concept that I could give to students who up to that time had been able to see only the figure of the man Jesus when I spoke of the Christ. The term I used was the Infinite Invisible. The words "Infinite Invisible" did for the students what the term "the Christ" had done for me. It took away all concepts.

The Christ to me has no form. The Christ cannot be visualized; the Christ can only be experienced. There is no way that I can define the Christ, picture It, circumscribe or limit It. So it is also with the term the Infinite Invisible.

If ever there are two words that cannot be bounded by the human mind, they are Infinite and Invisible. When we have a concept of God which breaks all bonds of limitation, separates it from all sense of sectarianism—Hebrew, Christian, Mohammedan, or Buddhist—a concept of God has been conveyed which is unlimited, infinite, eternal, universal Being. After each person himself has the experience of God, he is not concerned with any name for God because now he knows Him as He is.

Let God Announce Itself

Sometimes students write, "I've realized that I am God." But that could not be true. We can say, "God is my being; God constitutes my being"; but to turn around and say that we constitute God's being is a little bit far-fetched. If we understood the Word *I* correctly that would be different. But if we did, we would never make the statement, "I am God."

The statement, "I am God," cannot be voiced: it can only be heard. When the voice announces within us, "Be still, and know that I am God,"[8] that verily is God. But the moment we say, "I am God," that cannot be. We need to be watchful lest we attempt to make a human being God or even to feel that the spiritual identity of a person constitutes the allness of the Godhead. Yet the allness of the Godhead does constitute individual being, and that you will have to wrestle with in your meditation.

The voice often comes and says to us, "Know ye not, *I* am God." The Master understood that when he said, "I and my Father are one,"[9] implying that the Father was greater than he. There was no duality or twoness there. It was only the degree of Consciousness announcing Itself.

We consider ourselves human beings, but then we realize, "No, we aren't, and we never were human beings." At first we may read about our divine sonship in a book and declare, "I am the child of God, the son of God." Later we may even come into the consciousness of that truth. Still later we may say, "I am the Christ," a very great claim to make, but it can become true. The day can come when the "still small voice"[10] announces, *"I* in the midst of you am the Christ."

There is no reason why that awareness cannot go on and on until we hear, as the Master did, "He that hath seen me hath seen the Father.[11]... for I and my Father are one." When this higher Consciousness takes over and speaks through us, It may truly say, *"I* am God." But let us be watchful that we do not say it out of the mind or with the lips. If it should ever cross our lips, let us be sure that it has been pushed through by an inner voice, an inner Selfhood, and that it has not been impelled by our conscious thinking.

A Higher Concept of Prayer

If we are wise and if we have the listening ear, we will be gaining higher and higher concepts of God and of prayer, until all concepts disappear and the experience of God takes their place. When that day arrives, a realization comes that regardless of what one has thought about God, it is not true, never was true, and represented only our degree of spiritual awareness at that particular moment.

It is the same with prayer. It is shocking to look back on the forms of prayer we have known and practiced and to realize what concepts of both God and prayer we have entertained. That forces us ultimately to the realization that no prayer ever known will influence God, which is the primary purpose of most prayer. The idea is to get God to do something that God is not already doing, to get God to do something for someone whom God at the moment is neglecting. Prayer on the whole is accepted as a means of bringing about God's influence in our individual experience and in the experience of our nation or the world.

As a person begins to think of the many ways in which he has used prayer, and the purposes for which he has used prayer, he will come to understand why all these ideas of prayer and God represent only concepts within his being, having no relationship at all and not even distantly related to the truth of being.

There is a very good reason why so much metaphysical work does not bring forth fruit, and there is also a good reason why some students in The Infinite Way are not doing the healing work that should be done. It is never because of the teaching that students fail. It is because of the wrong concept of God and prayer that they entertain in spite of the revelation of God and prayer. Anyone opening his consciousness to truth ultimately will receive it, but the point to be watched is that we do not become frozen on somebody else's concept of prayer and somebody else's concept of God. John could say that God is love, but we do not know what he meant when he said that God is love. That immediately sets up some thought in us of what God is, of what love is, and that is where the error comes in. God is love, but God is not love when we think of God through our concepts of what love is.

Climbing Up to Higher Realms of Prayer

In order to go forward on the spiritual path it is necessary for us to find a way of shutting out our concepts, some way of arriving at the point in consciousness where we can say,

"I await within me the unfoldment of God and prayer," and find a way to keep out the intrusion of our former concepts of these subjects. Probably not one of us has risen high enough in the realization of God and prayer to be entirely satisfied with what we are showing forth in this experience. All of us must make progress in attaining a higher consciousness of God and a higher consciousness of prayer, but that will not be while we are entertaining concepts, ideas, thoughts, and beliefs about God and prayer.

Anything that we read or hear about God or prayer should serve the purpose of wiping out some of the old concepts and lift us into higher concepts, but even that is not the answer. The answer will come in the realization of the truth that whatever we are to know about God and prayer must reveal itself to us from within our own being. Let our work this year be that every person studying the letter may be lifted above the atmosphere of mind into the atmosphere of Soul, into the consciousness of the Soul-faculties so that he may be on a level from which this unfoldment can come, in other words, lifted into an atmosphere of consciousness where he can behold spiritual reality.

When we rise in consciousness to a height where we perceive the degree of unfoldment of Moses, Elijah, Elias, Isaiah, Jesus, or John, we catch the meaning of the statements, "God is love"; or "God is ever with us"; or "I will never leave you or forsake you." On our mortal, human level of consciousness, mixed a little with the spiritual level, we catch glimpses of what "I will never leave you, nor forsake you" means. It has an entirely different meaning once we apprehend it from the height of the Mount of Transfiguration. Then the real meaning of *I* dawns upon us, the *I* that goes with us, the *I* that goes through the waters so we do not drown, and through the flames, so that there will not even be the smell of smoke.

When the experience comes, life begins all over again. It could begin at forty or eighty or one hundred and twenty, but it begins again when that realization comes from the depth within us. So our real work this year will be climbing that Mount of Transfiguration until we reach a height of consciousness in which Spirit defines Itself to us, Spirit reveals Itself to us in infinite form and variety. It will not wipe out individuality: it will show forth the immortality of individuality because it will reveal to us the Elijah-state of consciousness, the Moses-state and the Elias-state of consciousness of thousands of years ago. It will reveal within our own being the same state of consciousness here and now that existed in Galilee or back in the Holy Lands thousands of years ago, and before that way back into India thousands of years before that. It will reveal the immortality of individual individuality. That is the miracle of true spiritual realization.

It is sad when some of our students say that since there is nobody to heal let us stop the healing work and declare that we are already in heaven. We are already in heaven, but so was the Prodigal Son still the son of his Father, although outwardly he was not manifesting his degree of sonship. He acknowledged that he was having less than his Father's servants. We today are having much less than our Father's servants but only because we have not yet attained the sonship-degree, much less the Fatherhood-degree. So while it is true that we are not going any place and that we are already there, let us acknowledge that Consciousness is unfolding and disclosing and revealing the infinite nature of Its being progressively and continuously.

Since no concept of God or prayer can be true, let us know that the truth about God and prayer must reveal itself to us from within our consciousness. It is the work of withdrawing concepts that God may announce Itself to us. That is our work this year and always until conscious union with God is attained.

Across the Desk

Living Between Two Worlds[12] was first begun by Joel while waiting for a plane at the airport in Seattle, Wash., in July of 1951, but it did not come to fruition until 1964 in a series of classes held in Hawaii. It points the way to living the spiritual life in a troubled and problem-ridden world. You will enjoy every word of it and find it meat and manna for today.

Tape Recorded Excerpts
Prepared by the Editor

Correctly understood, the personal relationship between a student and teacher, when a teacher has accepted a student for special work, is a very unique and beautiful one. Sometimes the personal nature of that relationship is misunderstood, but the following excerpts from a tape recording should help to clarify this subject.

Personal or Impersonal

"I have found in the ten years in which I have been teaching this message that my relationship with the students is not impersonal. There is something very, very personal about it, personal in the sense that with every student who brings himself to my attention his life becomes important. I glory in every step of spiritual unfoldment that he experiences and every bit of fruitage that comes into his life, and when he is struggling toward that, it is my joy to work with him, whether in person, as I have done with many with whom I have had the opportunity to be present, or by mail, and those who have experienced that know that there is no limit to the amount of letter writing that I can do when the occasion warrants it and when the student is able to accept the instruction, even if sometimes it comes in a very severe way.

"All of that to me is personal. In the same way when students are going through difficulties, that becomes personal to me, and I go far out of my way to help them through those periods and to stand by with them. And it is just as personal with me when they fall by the wayside, as some inevitably do. I am sure that there was nothing impersonal in the relationship between Jesus Christ and his disciples and apostles and the two hundred. I am sure that his teaching and his relationship with them was both close and personal. I am sure when he saw Judas about to fall away that he grieved in a very personal way, too, not only for his own life, but for what he knew Judas would have to go through to get back on the beam again. Having had three years with Judas, I am convinced that he knew that Judas was made of good stuff, that Judas Iscariot had deep spiritual possibilities and potentialities and that, therefore, he knew that eventually Judas was going to be back in the fold.

"I am sure that he must have grieved as he stood there and saw Peter hiding, Peter denying him. … That was a very personal feeling, and not for himself, but for Peter. And I'm sure that he must have rejoiced in a very personal way when he saw Peter come back into the fold so quickly and show as clearly as he did that it was a momentary aberration with him and one quickly to be forgotten.

"The spiritual teachers whom I have met around the world feel a deep love for their students, a deep rejoicing in those that prosper spiritually and a deep regret for those who do not seem to have a capacity to grasp the meaning of the spiritual way of life. It has always been that way with me. As a matter of fact, I am aware of the fact that it is often said of me that I have pets, that I have favorites, and you may be assured... that it is true: I have. There has never been a time when I have not had favorites and pets, and I don't believe there ever will be a time.

"Having gone through deep struggles to achieve even a tiny measure of this spiritual light, I can remember clearly those practitioners and teachers who were faithful, loving, kind, generous in their work with me, I can remember the patience that some of them had to exercise with me because I was not an easy student. Knowing what I went through to achieve even a small measure, I have that same feeling every time I see a student anywhere trying to break through this mesmeric sense, this personal sense of self. It is for that reason that when I find students struggling with sincerity, it is my joy to work harder with them, and perhaps outwardly seem to be making a pet of them. Really, it is not so much making a pet of them as it is giving them that additional time or effort that they may require at some particular point of their unfoldment. ...

"To me this teaching is personal. It is not impersonal. It has to do with an individual who today is a teacher working with one who today is a student, meeting on the level of the Spirit, of the Soul, thereby forming a bond greater than any human relationship that has ever been known. It is closer than any relationship that exists between man and wife or parent and child. It is a deeper relationship because it has in it none of the personal sense of selfishness that sometimes, too often, comes into those relationships of man and wife and parent and child. There is no sense of self in it and the reason is that neither teacher nor student gains anything of a temporal nature from that contact for spiritual unfoldment. They receive only the Spirit and the fruits of the Spirit, and it is not something that they receive so much as something that they in turn give or impart to others. ... This relationship that becomes so personal becomes beautiful because neither one can personally benefit by it. It requires a greater sacrifice both on the part of the teacher and the student because of the greater demands that are made upon them through the very activity of the Christ functioning in their consciousness. ... So it is in our relationship with each other, let us not be afraid to make it personal."

> Joel S. Goldsmith, "The Fruit of the Art of Meditation,"
> *The 1957 Chicago Open Class.*

❖ 3 ❖

THE NATURE OF
SPIRITUAL DISCERNMENT

SPIRITUALLY THE WORLD is embodied within our consciousness. We live in a world of mountains, valleys, streams, rivers, and oceans, sun, moon, and stars. We live in a world of warmth and ice, but in whatever part of the world we live, we react to "this world"[1] in terms of our own state of consciousness. There is in reality no good or evil in the world: the world is made up of mountains, valleys, rivers, oceans, trees, sun, moon, and stars, but it is not good and it is not bad, nor any degree in between.

When those who live in Hawaii exclaim, "How wonderful life is in these Hawaiian Islands, with the beauty, climate, foliage, ocean, and mountains," they are investing the Islands with qualities of good. There are those from other states who would not find Hawaii quite so good: they would miss the snow, the ice, the cool air, the snappy, chilly evenings, and the brisk mornings. There are even some who respond to a warm climate such as that of Hawaii by becoming ill, and there are others who respond to it by becoming well. In other words, health is not to be found in any climate, in any country, or in any state: health is an attitude of mind, a state of consciousness, and a person responds to a place in accord with his state of consciousness.

All this is a part of the state of consciousness that we brought into this world or that we took on through our environment or education. This constitutes being not only *in* this world but *of* this world. We are responding to appearances and beliefs. We find beauty in things, persons, or circumstances where there is no beauty, and we find ugliness where there is no ugliness, all because we are responding to universal belief.

Do Not Judge by Appearances

In the spiritual life, we are told to "judge not according to the appearance."[2] This does not mean that we are merely to judge not negative appearances, but judge not any appearance. The Master said, "Why callest thou me good? there is none good but one, that is, God."[3] How careful he was to turn his followers away from every appearance in order that they might have the experience!

But how do we attain the experience of living in the world and yet not being of it, that is, not being subject unto it? We do that through an activity of our consciousness. We withdraw good and evil from the appearance. Let me illustrate that. As we look out at a group of people we recognize that in the human picture some are good and some not so good; some are well and others not so well, some are young and some not so young. These are all appearances. If we live in the world and are of it, we accept these appearances at face value. But if we are on the spiritual path all this must change. We must look out at a group or at any person and realize, "There is neither good nor evil before me, neither sickness nor health, neither youth nor age, neither sin nor purity."

We can do this only if we do not judge by appearances, if we can set our emotions aside so that we do not just like the ones we like, and dislike the ones we think we may not like. We have to put all this aside and agree, "God made all that was made, but with my human eyes I cannot see God's creation. I cannot see you as you are in God, that is, not with my eyes, nor can I know what you are like as the image and likeness of God. Therefore, whether with my eyes open or closed, I must shut out the picture of you as my eyes would see you, as my emotions would like to think of you, and I must turn within and pray, 'Father, reveal to me man in Your image and likeness, the manifestation of Your own being.'"

Spiritual Discernment Reveals What Is

In the very moment that we have decided not to judge by appearances, we have set something within us in the direction of the development of the Soul-faculty of spiritual discernment. We have established an agreement within ourselves that what we see, hear, taste, touch, and smell has nothing to do with a person as he is, and we have agreed within ourselves that we cannot judge him by any of the human standards of the five physical senses. Therefore we must wait on God; we must wait for spiritual discernment to reveal him to us as he is.

We have opportunities for the practice of this all day long and all night long, first, because it is necessary that we come to know the members of our own family as they are rather than as they appear to be. We never will be entirely satisfied with them as they humanly appear to be. True happiness can come only in discerning the real nature of what is hidden from view. As we practice this, some come to us and ask for help, for our prayers.

A healing consciousness knows that a human being is not what he appears to be; it knows that we cannot see, hear, taste, touch, or smell a person as he is in God's image and likeness and that we cannot judge him by any standard of the human mind. We must, therefore, wait for a spiritual faculty to develop within us that enables us to discern man or some particular man, woman, or child in the image and likeness of God.

In order to attain the consciousness of no judgment, we must do this with cats, dogs, trees, mountains, and oceans. We must stop loving oceans just because our nature may happen to be one that enjoys being close to the sea. We must stop loving mountains just because our nature happens to be one that responds to being in high places, and we must begin to discern the mountains and the sea from God's standpoint. God did not make a mountain for some people to like and some to dislike; God did not make a sea to be magnificent to some and destructive to others; God did not make trees to bless some and not others. All that God made is good.

Attaining the Garden-of-Eden State of Consciousness

There are many persons who do not like cats and many who do not like dogs, and some who do not like animals at all. Certainly there are many who fear reptiles and wild beasts, but on the spiritual path we cannot remain in the world and *of* it: we must remain in it but not be of it. We do not have to go out into the wilds and face reptiles or beasts physically, but right where we are, we face the part of the world that we like and the part that we do not like, and realize, "There is more to you than the eye beholds, and until I have developed the capacity of spiritual discernment, I will not know man or animal as he is in God, nor will I know the world as it is in God, and therefore I will never know what it is to live in the Garden of Eden."

The Garden of Eden does not exist in time; the Garden of Eden does not exist in space; and it does not even exist in the future for us. There is no place where we can find it, not even in some spots on the face of the globe where it is claimed the Garden of Eden once was. The truth is that the Garden of Eden was never in any particular place because the Garden of Eden is a state of divine consciousness. We live in It here and now in proportion as we can discern the nature and character of man as he is in the image and likeness of God and as we can discern the mountains, valleys, trees, streams, and oceans as they are as God's creation.

God's creation is spiritual. As the inner faculty of discernment is developed we will begin to see spiritually, hear spiritually, and know spiritually, all of which constitutes discernment. "Have I been so long time with you, and yet hast thou not known me, Phillip?"[4] "Whom do men say that I the Son of man am? … But whom say ye that I am?"[5] Are we seeing Jesus as a man? Are we seeing our husband, our wife, or our child as man, woman, or child, or do we have eyes that really see? Do we have ears that really hear? Do we have a power of discernment that transcends the five physical senses?

On this point hinges the entire spiritual life, and on this point hinges spiritual healing. With the five physical senses, that is, with the human mind, we would be more than foolish if we stated that there is no sin, disease, or death in the world, or if we were to say there is no lack, limitation, or stupidity. Once spiritual discernment has been attained, even in a small measure, however, we begin to perceive God's creation right where mortality appears to be, and this constitutes the healing consciousness. The difference between a student who is doing spiritual healing work and the rest of the world is that those doing healing work have attained enough of spiritual discernment to see through the appearance to the world, the man, and the law of God's creating, whereas the world as a whole judges entirely by appearances.

No Destruction in God's Creation

God never created a destructive law. In reality there is no such thing as a law of disease or a law of death. To attain our freedom from these means to attain the power of spiritual discernment, so that we can see the nature of God's law, and in the presence of that power of discernment, the material sense of law evaporates.

All the evils of this world are man-created, that is, they are mind-created. They are the creation of that which is called the Lord God, or law. It is the mistaken belief that this law, or Lord God, was God that has resulted in the slavery of the entire world—physical, mental, moral, and financial slavery—and all because the ancient Hebrew Scriptures that spoke of God and a Lord God were interpreted as if both terms meant God, and they do not. The Lord God is the law, and this law is done away with in Christ.

Sooner or later the world will realize that the law and God are not the same. The law has to do with as-ye-sow-so-shall-ye-reap, but there is no such law in God. In God there is forgiveness seventy times seven. In God there is not as-ye-sow-so-shall-ye-reap, and it serves you right. Rather, there is, "'Neither do I condemn thee,'[6] I forgive thee. I do not judge or condemn thee. I set thee free." So all that has been accepted as the good and evil of God is an error. Only those who realize the nature of God as immortal Being can understand that there can be no destruction in God or the creation of God: no beginning to it, no ending to it. It is a state of immortality.

Spiritual Healing, an
Activity of Spiritual Discernment

Since we were born into the human mind with its belief in good and evil and into the belief that there are God-laws of good and evil, we cannot rise above them except by a conscious act of our consciousness, consciously withdrawing good and evil from this world and its people, and then saying, "Father, I know not how to pray; I know not how to judge; I know not how to understand; I know not how to go out or come in. 'Speak, Lord; for thy servant heareth.'"[7] By living constantly in that attitude of receptivity, God speaks through us and within us, revealing His creation. That is all there is to spiritual healing.

When someone has presented the appearance of a sick mind, a sick body, or a sick pocketbook, and someone of spiritual discernment has seen through the appearance, has let himself live in the world but not of it, and has not accepted the world's judgments, then the grace of God comes through as light, and there is no darkness any more. In His presence is freedom; in His presence is divine Grace; in His presence is liberation. The spiritual healer is one whose consciousness is open to let the still small voice utter Itself so that the earth of error may melt.

We build the capacity of spiritual discernment as we agree that God's universe is wholly good and wholly spiritual. With our eyes we cannot believe this, nor with our

ears. Our mind will never convince us of this, because our
mind is seeing, hearing, tasting, touching, and smelling too
much of evil. Therefore, we must be still; we must attain
quietness and peace and the ability to live in that attitude
so that instead of indulging our likes and dislikes, instead of
judging by appearances, we let the spiritual faculty within
us discern the nature of that which is appearing to us and
being revealed to us. Then It ultimately tells us, "This is My
son, in whom *I* am well pleased." When the voice says that,
light has appeared and the darkness goes, and someone says,
"I am healed."

We Have No Power to Give or Withhold Healing

God does not give, and God does not withhold. We
have no right to believe that we can give good to anyone,
even good health, or that we can withhold it from another.
We can neither give nor withhold: we can only discern. The
manner in which this discernment operates must have a great
deal to do with some inner receptivity on the part of those
who come within range of our consciousness, because we are
constantly having mystifying experiences.

At one time a student wrote me a letter calling my
attention to a man in a hospital who the doctors said could
not possibly live. There was no hope for him. It was a very
distressing case, and the story had so touched the student
that she wanted to give help, but did not feel capable of it
and wrote to ask if I would help this man. The man knew
nothing about her request and nothing about the nature of
our work, so my answer had to be: I can neither give nor
withhold. There is no doubt that my inner discernment
says to me that this man, like myself and like everyone, is

God's image and likeness, the very representation on earth of God's own being. I know that, but I cannot give that to him and I cannot withhold it from him: it is the truth about him. To what extent he receives healing, I have no way of knowing. I believe that it will have something to do with his own discernment.

Shortly thereafter I received a newspaper clipping from the student. The man was healed, and the doctors could not understand what had happened: "All we can say is, it might happen again, but we do not know how it happened this time." I still maintain that I cannot give, and I cannot withhold, but I can discern, and then perhaps the degree of a person's receptivity determines what takes place after that discernment.

When we are called upon for help, we cannot give healing, and we cannot withhold healing, but if we are developing the inner capacity of spiritual discernment, we can discern the nature of the image and likeness of God, and then in proportion to the measure of receptivity, there is healing. It may be an instantaneous healing or it may be long-drawn-out.

Receptivity Comes by Grace

Receptivity is not something over which we have control. We cannot blame anyone for a lack of receptivity, nor can we give credit to anyone who has receptivity, because it is not of him: it is of God. If my own will, desire, or hope could be fulfilled, my receptivity would be so tremendous that I would be the full and complete Christ, but I cannot give that to myself and I cannot withhold it from myself. I have to wait as patiently as any other person must wait for the Spirit to move upon the face of the waters. We have to wait for the

Spirit to open us from the bud that we are when we come to this work to the full-blown flower that eventually we will be.

This full measure of receptivity has not yet taken place within me or within you. I cannot help it; you cannot help it. I can do only one thing and that is to be as faithful to what I understand as I can be, and then wait patiently for further Grace to unfold within me. So it is with you; so it is with all of us. We know that Christhood, the full Christhood, is the measure of our being. We also know that we cannot claim to have fully attained, but since we know the goal and since we know the only way of attainment is the further development of this spiritual capacity of discernment, we know that it involves practice, practice, constant practice.

The Middle Path

Fortunately, throughout our waking hours and in a measure carrying over into our sleeping hours, we have the opportunity and the capacity consciously to remember every time we invest anything with a quality of good, immediately to withdraw that judgment and say, "No, no, Father, reveal to me the true quality." Every time we invest anything or anybody with any quality of humanhood, positive or negative, we can withdraw it and turn to this power of discernment that is within and ask for light. Then we will receive light on its true nature and, as this develops, by beholding more and more of Christhood, we become more and more of the Christ.

In The Infinite Way this is called the middle path: neither good humanhood nor bad humanhood, but spirituality; neither healthy humanhood nor sickly humanhood, but spirituality; neither young age, old age, nor middle age, but eternal agelessness, immortality. In other words, we are withdrawing the qualities of good and evil, up and down, sick and well, rich and poor; we are withdrawing all of this and then letting spiritual discernment reveal to us the spiritual nature of creation.

Illumination Brings
Spiritual Discernment

Illumination is really the power of the spiritual discernment of an individual, and it is this that brings healing: not *a* God, not *the* God, not God. Only the developed or natural spiritual discernment of an individual performs the miracle.

Moses and many of the Hebrew prophets healed before there was such a thing as Christianity. Five hundred years before Jesus there was a tremendous healing ministry across India in ashramas founded by the disciples of the Buddha. Jesus performed his healing works through his spiritual discernment, but not because there was a God that would do something for Jesus that He would not do for someone else. What then performs the miracles? In proportion as our consciousness is illumined, which means in proportion as we develop the power of spiritual discernment, is everyone who comes within range of our consciousness blessed. Those who have the greatest spiritual receptivity receive the greatest benefit.

God is the same yesterday, today, and forever. God is the same for Hebrews, Hindus, Buddhists, and Christians. There is only one God, Omnipresence Itself, Omnipresence within us, the kingdom of God within. God is neither lo here, nor lo there; there is no God here or there. The kingdom of God is within us, and it manifests as spiritual discernment.

As we learn not to judge by appearances, but to withdraw all judgment and turn within and let this spiritual discernment reveal the nature of the world, we discover that the world is not this world: it is My kingdom. My kingdom is not up in heaven, and this world is not down on earth. Whether we are living in this world or in the heaven of My kingdom depends not on going some place sometime, but on the degree of spiritual discernment that is developed within us. This determines the degree of heaven we experience; the lack of it determines the degree of hell.

Only Those With a Measure of the Christ Can Behold the Christ

"I and my Father are one"[8] is a universal relationship, but looking at the human race, we could never believe it. This is because the human race is not one with God or it would be God-governed and God-maintained. In proportion as we do not judge after appearances but turn within and let the grace of God reveal the nature of what is appearing to us is the Son of God raised up in us and in every person. The more of the Christ I can behold in a person the greater is the degree of Christ that has been raised up in me. Only through the Christ of me can I behold the Christ of you.

When Peter acknowledged, "Thou art the Christ, the Son of the living God,"[9] the Master could say to Peter, "'Flesh and blood hath not revealed it unto thee, but my Father which is in heaven.'[10] You have not been able to discern this of yourself. It is the Father within you, the power of spiritual discernment within you, that has enabled you to behold the Christ of me."

That is why he could take three of his disciples to the Mount of Transfiguration.[11] Those who had attained the highest degree of spiritual discernment could behold the incorporeal omnipresence of the Hebrew prophets who had left this earth plane hundreds of years before. They could discern that the prophets had not gone anywhere, that they were still here, omnipresent, and the disciples could still tabernacle with them.

All the seers, all those who have attained Christhood, are still with us. We do not see them with the physical eye, but we will discern them with spiritual discernment, and sometimes that will be so real that we can actually believe we are seeing them with the physical eye.

Our Hidden Spiritual Capacity Is Always Seeking an Outlet

Spiritual discernment is a capacity that is given to all of us, but which lies buried deep within us through centuries of human experience. Now we are bringing it to the surface and discovering a capacity we never knew we had.

I knew a man who was so unhappy in his childhood that at nine years of age he ran away from home. He worked his way to a foreign country and engaged in farming activity until well up into the teens. Then he discovered that he had a great musical talent and later became a famous conductor, composer, and arranger, living out the balance of his days as an outstanding musical light. Think what that boy had hidden inside of him awaiting recognition, probably surrounded by a family who could never understand it, never agree with it, and never gave it the opportunity of coming out. Not knowing why or what was going on within him, he had to run away from home and give this talent an opportunity to come into expression, which it ultimately did.

Probably every person has experienced unhappiness, frustration, and discontent in a measure. Being healthy or sick, wealthy or poor has nothing to do with it. Health does not bring "the peace... which passeth all understanding,"[12] and neither does wealth. A spiritual capacity is hidden within every person, and it has been seeking outlet almost from the day he came on earth. Because it has not been given the opportunity of expression, it sets up a battle within a person, making him think sometimes that he needs health, at other times that he needs wealth or fame. Always he needs some outlet that he has not found. Some had to have marriage, and some had to have divorce. Why? Because the person was seeking something, not realizing that it was not he seeking anything: it was this hidden spiritual capacity seeking an outlet.

Seek Within

We must begin to relax from seeking our happiness in the outside world, seeking it through persons, circumstances, or conditions, and acknowledge, "There is a kingdom of God within me, a kingdom I have not yet come to know or experience. There is a capacity of spiritual awareness, spiritual discernment, within me that would let me see this world as it is." Then, as we learn to live in this withinness only a few periods a day of a few minutes each, it expands of itself into more minutes and more periods. But give this inner capacity, this inner power of spiritual discernment, an opportunity to come out.

Everyone has spiritual discernment. That is why the Master could pick his disciples from fishermen and tax collectors. He knew that everyone has it, and he could teach them how to stop taking thought for their fish and their fishermen's nets and tell them, "Follow me, and I will make you fishers of men."[13] That is the message of the Master: to stop being concerned about the outer affairs of life. Then in a moment that we know not, in a moment we are at peace, this power of spiritual discernment will spring into active being, and we will see as we are seen by God. We will see the Christ as God sees the Christ. We will even come to know Jesus in a far different way than we have ever known him before, because when we see Jesus through spiritual discernment, we will come face to face with the fullness of illumination.

This fullness has probably only been evidenced three times in the history of the world, but we will find it when the Spirit, that "mind... which was also in Christ Jesus,"[14] is awakened in us. We will then see as we are seen by God, and we will see ourselves as Jesus the Christ in the Holy Land saw all mankind. He could put out his hands and say, "O Jerusalem... how often would I have gathered thy children together, even as a hen gathereth her chickens under her wings, and ye would not!"[15]

If we could have seen the physical appearance of those to whom he was speaking, we would wonder how he could have had such compassion, how he could have had such tenderness and love, since they were resisting him and rebelling. But through that great capacity of spiritual discernment, he could behold the Christ in them longing to come out into expression.

Spiritual Discernment
Sets the Individual Free

Jesus had no thought, as the Hebrews of old had, of merely improving their humanhood. He discarded nine of the Ten Commandments, because he knew that even if they obeyed those nine Commandments, they would just be human beings on a little higher level, and they could retrograde, which has happened all through history. But if he could arouse and awaken in them the power of spiritual discernment, the capacity to know, to see, and to hear spiritually, to behold spiritually, never again would they be in subjection to the temple, to the synagogue, to Caesar, or even to the physical body.

Spiritual discernment deprives us of a great deal of emotion and sensuality. Sometimes we wonder if there is anything to take the place of these emotions that are no longer a part of us. But indeed there is. With the spiritual capacity comes an awareness of God's universe, God's man, and God's body, which far transcends any human sense of joy or beauty that the mind can know.

We are called upon to leave our nets, to leave the physical sense of universe, sun, moon, stars, mountains, seas, and human body, and come unto *Me*, and see as *I* see, hear as *I* hear, discern as *I* do the spiritual nature of this universe, and then find that heaven is established on earth.

Across the Desk

Many aspects of The Infinite Way may appear to be paradoxical. For example, we are taught that we do not work for a living. Therefore, sometimes students think that the highest spiritual attainment is evidenced by just sitting and doing nothing and waiting for food, housing, and clothing to come to them, hopefully expecting others to provide for them and not really relying on the one Source. Instead of giving evidence of spiritual attainment, in many cases such students are showing forth a parasitical state of consciousness.

The deeper a student's realization, the more work is given him to do and the busier he becomes. Joel was a perfect example of this principle of life. Far from being able to rest back and spend his days in contemplation to the exclusion of all else, he found himself busier than ever with each passing day.

The Infinite Way is a way of life in the world in which the demands of this world are fulfilled while yet maintaining more consistently than ever before that inner reliance and awareness. God is forever expressing as individual being, expressing as infinite forms of activity. Did not Jesus, when still a child, say, "Wist ye not that I must be about my Father's business,"[16] and later, "My Father worketh hitherto, and I work"?[17] So we, too, must let the Spirit find expression through us by beginning to do the work at hand whether we like it or whether it appears to be appropriate or not.

TAPE RECORDED EXCERPTS
Prepared by the Editor

Now there are diversities of gifts, but the same Spirit.

I Corinthians 12:4

To each of us is given a talent and a work to do in the world. What that work is to be we never discover while looking only at our experience, education, and background, judging our contribution to the world in those terms and accepting their limitations. The gift of God flows forth from within our being, and as we learn to turn within for guidance, direction, and fulfillment, always beginning by doing the work at hand, the way is opened for developing and putting into use our divine capacity. The way is pointed out so clearly in the following excerpt:

Finding Our Place in the World

"'Why am I on earth? Why was I born? Why do I continue to take up space on this earth? What is the purpose? What is the function that I am to perform in being here?' If you try to answer from any human standpoint, you will be wrong. You are not here in order that you may be a wife, a husband, a mother, or a father; you are not here that you may be successful in business, art, or a profession. You are not here that you may accomplish good on earth.

"You are here for only one purpose, and that is that God's purpose be fulfilled in you, not your purpose. Regardless of how good and how noble it might be, if it is your purpose, you are wrong. ... Put yourself aside and realize: 'God created me for His purpose, not mine. God created me to perform His will on earth, not for me... to decide what I want to be, what I want to do, and where I want to do it.' That would be having a mind apart from God, a will apart from God. ...

"'Let me know Thy will, and I will follow it. Make Thy will evident in me. Lead me in the way that Thou wishest me to go. Let me on earth be a fulfillment of Thy plan; let me on earth be the showing forth of Thy glory, so that wherever I go it will be said, "There is the presence of God. How wonderful is the presence of God!" And let not attention be called to the personal accomplishments of an individual. '...

"Our will, our plan, our hopes, our ambitions—even when they are good, even when they are noble—must be put aside in order that we become a transparency for God. ..."

Joel S. Goldsmith, "The Soul of Man,"
The 1961 Hawaiian Village Open Class.

❋ 4 ❋

IMMORTALITY UNVEILED

IT IS NOT possible to enter into the Christ-consciousness while you are trying to change appearances. Evil becomes less operative in your life, however, as you rise to a place in consciousness where you recognize that God is Spirit, that Spirit alone is power, and that there is no power aside from Spirit—not that there is not a claim of material and mental power in the human world. But you cannot change that until you rise above the material and mental levels into the spiritual, and it is there that you will recognize the illusory nature of all so-called powers. Actually, it is impossible for an illusion to create any real thing. All it can create is a mental image in thought.

The world is the temple of God. It is not an illusion even though some Oriental teachings claim it is. The illusion is in our sense of the world. But what has happened to those who have accepted this world as an illusion? "By their fruits ye shall know them."[1] Has there been clearly identifiable fruitage?

God never created an illusion, and God did create the world which to human sense is seen "through a glass darkly."[2] If only it could be seen face to face, this very universe would be the temple of God, as your individual body would be. Your body is the temple of God, but you are seeing it through the universal belief in two powers, and the sooner you come to some measure of realization of one power, the sooner will

your body begin to respond. As you learn this principle of
The Infinite Way, you will disregard appearances, knowing
that you are witnessing these appearances through the illusory sense of the belief in two powers.

Impersonal Nature of Error Makes
Healing Relatively Easy

Infinite Way work is carried on entirely from the standpoint that all evil, regardless of its name or nature, is impersonal and has its source in a universal belief in two powers. It
is for this reason that you never take the name of the patient
or the disease into your treatment. You are not dealing with
persons or disease: you are dealing with a universal illusion,
the Adamic dream, the carnal mind. Call it what you will, in
the end it has to be recognized as nonpower.

To be able to heal through The Infinite Way, you must
first of all understand that God appears as men and women.
You and I are the manifestation of all that God is, God in
expression. You do not express God: God expresses Himself
as you. God is doing the expressing, not you. You do not have
the ability to express God. God alone expresses God. God
expresses Himself as you, but it is God doing the expressing,
God doing the living. You are not living God's life. God is
living His life through you if you will stop taking thought
for your life. God is doing the thinking: you are not thinking
God's thoughts. God is thinking God's thoughts through
you if you are receptive.

This is the truth of being. Any appearance to the contrary is based on the universal belief in two powers, entirely
impersonal; and because it was not created by God, it has
no power and no law to sustain it. Because The Infinite Way
recognizes the impersonal nature of error and then dispels it

through the recognition of its nothingness, with almost all the ills of mankind there will probably be eighty percent of very quick healings. The other claims that last longer have been absorbed into consciousness personally. For one reason or another, patients have hugged the particular beliefs to them that do not readily yield.

The moment most persons pass seventy, they begin to accept "threescore years and ten."[3] They apply it as a law to themselves; they begin to fear the ills which universal belief has fastened on the years after seventy, and then they experience them. Other persons have been brought up to fear poverty, and they live so in that fear that they end up destitute. Others fear cancer or heart disease. Why? Because they hear so much about them, and in that way hug them to themselves, and give a practitioner a hard time to free them. They, themselves, have personalized them. With eighty percent of the claims, however, most persons not only do not want any part of them, but they do not fear them, and as long as they do not love, hate, or fear them, the practitioner has any easy time with them. There has arisen such a world of fear of certain diseases that long before persons get them they are fearing them, so what they are doing is preparing the soil in which they can take root. Then it is more difficult to weed them out.

Healing should be a very simple thing. It involves the ability not to react to appearances; it involves the ability to realize: I am not dealing with a condition that has to be fought or overcome.

A Human Being Cannot Be Spiritualized

A human being cannot be spiritual; a human being cannot be God or the Christ. But in proportion as the human being dies to his humanhood, Christhood is more and more revealed, sometimes more to the onlooker than to the individual himself. That probably explains why a mystic cannot claim to be a mystic. Do you not see that in the moment that a person has experienced the Christ he has beheld perfection, and from that moment on he is comparing himself with that perfection? Do you see how unworthy he must become in his own eyes? Even while others may say, "He has improved," or "He is a better man," the individual himself cannot feel that, because he is always measuring himself against the perfection he has experienced, and he knows how far from that he is. So Jesus could say, "Why callest thou me good? there is none good but one, that is God."[4] A man walking the earth cannot say, "I am the Christ." That really is sinful. But for a person to know that the Christ is his identity is quite another matter, and forgetting his past sins, he looks forward to attaining the realization of that Christhood.

If you hear within you, "Thou art my son in whom I am well pleased. Be still and know that *I* am God," you are hearing aright. That gives you no privilege to say those words, because in the saying of them, you reverse the meaning. The moment you say that you are the Christ, you have lost It. It is only when you hear the "still small voice"[5] say those words that you are hearing truth. When you say, "I am Christ"; "I am Spirit"; "I am God"; you are trying to immortalize a human being, and you have only to look in the mirror to find out that you are lying. But when that still, small voice says to you, "This is my beloved Son, in whom I am well pleased,"[6] even though that person may at the moment appear to be dying or in dire need, you know that God has spoken to him and revealed his true identity. Then there must come a healing.

The ideal way of living is to be in the world but not of it and to perform all the functions of your business or profession and still not be of it. No one should believe that the spiritual life is intended to set him apart in a monastery or convent. The function of the spiritual life is to bring your spiritual influence into the world. Yes, go up to the mountaintop for forty days and nights to be inspired of God, but then come down to the plains and the seaside and heal the sick, forgive the sinners, raise the dead, and feed the hungry. To enable the student individually to rise so high in consciousness that he recognizes God as the central theme of the universe, and all evil as merely the impersonal belief in two powers, and thereby nothingizes it, is the function of this work.

God As Individual Being

In the beginning, God, and God sent Himself forth into expression as man. God, the Father, appeared individually as God, the son. You can understand that more readily if you think of the sun in the sky and then think of the sunbeams. The sun—the great big, universal sun—is manifesting itself as sunbeams. Each sunbeam is made up of all that the sun is made up of: light, warmth, and whatever else there is to the sun. So you can see that God, the Infinite, Omnipotent, Omniscient, Omnipresent sends Himself forth as the Son, individual you and me. But it is still God, and the individual has all the qualities of the Father. "Son, thou art ever with me, and all that I have is thine."[7]

The sun is saying to the sunbeam, "Sunbeam, you have all that I have. You have the light that I am, and you have the warmth that I am. We are one." So God says, "I am God, the Father. You are God, the son. All that *I* have is thine. All My qualities are your qualities. My life is your life. You have no life of your own: the only life you are living is My life. You have no mind of your own: the only mind you have is My mind. You have no soul of your own: the only soul you have is My Soul. *I* am God, the Father; you are God, the son; and we are really one. *I* have manifested Myself on earth as you." All this is in the beginning, and this is your spiritual identity, your true Selfhood. This is what you are; this is what I am now in this very moment.

Somewhere along the line there arose a mist—that is one way of putting it; or Adam and Eve sinned—that is another way of putting it; or man fell—that is still another way of putting it. It means that we forgot our identity, our Father. We look in the mirror, or we look in the lake or the river and see a reflection and say, "Oh, that is I." Then we think that is all there is to us, forgetting that what we are seeing is only the body, the form. But there is more to us than body and form. Recognizing ourselves only as body and form, we live more or less on the animal level, dominated by animal instincts.

Through the centuries we have been working toward civilization, but for the most part we have just been animal beings, human, human beings: bad human beings becoming good human beings, imperialistic human beings becoming democratic or republican human beings. Only the few have made the jump out of mortality into immortality. Only a few had the vision to see that whether they are bad human beings or good human beings, they are still human. As long as a person is human, the good one can become bad, and the bad can become good, but he is still human.

Awakening to Your True Identity

It is only when enough light reaches your consciousness that you begin to perceive what the Master meant when he said, "My kingdom is not of this world.[8] ... I have meat to eat that ye know not of."[9] When you begin to question what the Master meant by "My kingdom," and the "meat to eat that ye know not of," through seeking and through bringing yourself into the atmosphere of those who have attained some measure of wisdom, either through personal contact or through their writings, a sentence here or a sentence there will awaken something in you, and suddenly you perceive that there is a hidden manna. Then you are getting somewhere. You are on the path of withinness, on the path of the inner kingdom.

As you continue, you arrive at a place where you realize, "Oh, there is Something more to me than 'me'. There is a Presence. I feel It. Sometimes It talks to me, sometimes It just directs or leads me, points the way in which I am to go. There is a 'me', but there is Something else, too. I am aware of some good coming into my experience that I did not earn, deserve, or prove worthy of; it just came by Grace. In many different ways I begin to see there is Something. In time It begins to impart Itself to me, and I recognize as Paul did that this Presence in me is really living my life."

By the time you get to a point where trouble was expected, the trouble is all gone. By the time you get to the place where you thought your supply would run out, you find a fresh supply. By the time you thought you had no friends, you make a new one. Something is going before you and doing strange and beautiful things in your life. Doors that were closed are opening; persons are appearing with a different opinion of you, a different thought of you. Something is happening.

You are aware now that a Presence goes before you to "make the crooked places straight,"[10] or a Presences goes with you and protects you. It may be in your car, driving; it may be anywhere; but all of sudden you have the assurance, "Fear not! Fear not! *I* am with you." You find that it is true, no matter what the danger is, no matter what the discord is, no matter what the misunderstanding is, it passes.

Scripture says, "Greater is he that is in you, than he that is in the world."[11] Now you are beginning to be aware there is a He within you. Whether Jesus calls It "the Father that dwelleth in me,"[12] or Paul calls it "the Christ indwelling," the name is not important. You know there is a Something, a Presence. It does wonderful things for you, and in proportion as you relax from taking thought for your life and stop fearing does this Presence take over more and more, until the day comes when someone may say to you, "Can I give you something? Can I lend you something? Can I do something for you?" Then you answer, "Oh, I have meat. I have all that is necessary," because now you have the understanding that you are one with the Father and all that the Father has is yours. From that moment your gaze is taken from the outer world, and you are no longer dependent on, "man, whose breath is in his nostrils."[13]

Living the Life of Withinness in Time of Lack

You may have to prove your freedom in a period of lack and limitation in which every human door shuts itself in your face. In fact, there was a time when every human door and every human avenue of supply were closed to me, and there I was. But believe me, there *I* was, also! It was in that period that the realization was given to me of this Presence, this "I and my Father are one,"[14] here where I stand. Even in that lack and limitation, there where I stood, I and the Father were one, and the realization of that broke the spell.

Probably up to that time in the back of my consciousness, I was blaming other people that they were not being a little more generous or were not doing things for me that they might have done, but at that moment I was able inwardly to say, "Keep everything you have. No longer do I need anything that any man has, 'I and my Father are one,' and mine is an unfolding good from within."

It still was very tough, because conditions did not change in a day, but within a few days they began to change very positively, but so gradually, so minutely. Although gradual, it was a steady upward and onward going, but always without looking to man, always without asking, always with the ability to rest back inside in the realization, "'I and my Father are one,' the *I* of my being is the incarnate Christ, the son of God; and It is my meat, my wine, and my water."

Spiritual Life Is a Dependence on the Within

The moment you enter into the life of withinness, which only begins when you recognize that there is a presence within, you withdraw your attention from the outer realm and more and more depend on the within. That does not mean that you become fanatical in your outer life; it does not mean that you throw up your job and sit on a park bench and wait to be supported. No, you go about your business or your profession, the same as you always have, only with the realization that you are serving: you are not expecting anything. You are giving and sharing: you are not asking for anything.

Let me put it another way. The appearance says that some form of justice or recognition is being withheld from you. You may be looking to someone, possibly a judge on a bench to hand out justice, and you will look in vain because it is not going to happen that way. Almost any lawyer will tell you not to go into court expecting justice. To settle your case before it gets to court is a safe policy to pursue whenever possible. But if you must go to court, do not look to the judge or the jury for justice. Go through the motions that are expected, but realize the only place from which justice can come is from within yourself. Nobody can give you justice, and no one can withhold justice from you because it is a part of your own Christhood; it is the meat you have that the world knows nothing of. Justice is a quality and an activity of your consciousness, and it does not come to you from anyone: it flows out from you to the world.

One of the greatest of all human mistakes is to think that someone owes you something. Nobody owes you anything because you have been Christed. God has incarnated His Son, the Christ, within you, and the Christ within is your meat, your wine, your water. You are to draw from the invisible source, from your hidden manna. It makes no difference whether it is money, recognition, reward, or justice.

When a person in the healing ministry has attained the consciousness of oneness with the Father and the consciousness that all that the Father has is his, he draws upon an invisible meat. There is then no need to make a charge for healing work because all that he needs comes in, sometimes through the practice in the form of gratitude tangibly expressed, and sometimes not. It comes, but the practitioner must have attained the consciousness of his union with God.

Just as now in Infinite Way healing work there is no specific charge, the day will come when there will be no need to make a charge for teaching. There would not be a need now, if all those who came to our work were far enough along on the spiritual path. It is only at the stage where the general public is still coming to us, those who have not yet ascended to the understanding of the nature of supply, of sharing, and gratitude, that there is a need in some departments of the work for specific charges.

While it is true that many persons never think of paying for spiritual help, and many sometimes pay what will not cover the postage, this insensitiveness and unwillingness to express gratitude tangibly is always on the part of those who have not yet come into any understanding of the spiritual life. They do not know what they are getting, and therefore they do not know what to give in exchange for it. The spiritual has no value in their experience.

Those who have a measure of spiritual light are more than generous in their sharing, and sharing as an expression of gratitude is important for a very good reason. How could a person—except the few who happen to be fortunately or sometimes unfortunately born to wealth—devote his life to this work and remain twenty-four hours a day, seven days a week, living in the Spirit, if he had to go out and battle the world competitively and then come home and engage in a healing ministry, and do as many of us do, have to be awake most of the night with telephone calls and cables? It just could not be. But as soon as an individual receives a measure of healing, and a degree of spiritual light opens in him, the first thing he wants to do is to share because he knows the value of what he has received.

A practitioner or a teacher in this work who has really been touched by the Spirit knows that he is not in a business: he is functioning only as an instrument to bring forth on earth the activity of God's grace which does not appear on earth except through individual consciousness. True, God's

grace was on earth before Jesus was, and he acknowledged
that the Christ was before Abraham. But of what avail was
that to sick people? Until an individual came along with a
Christ-consciousness, the healing consciousness, divine
grace was inoperative. What good was it to the sinners to
know that there was a God? None, until there was an individual who could be an inlet and an outlet for God's forgiving grace. What good would it do the people who were
hungry unless there were an individual who knew how to
multiply? In other words, all the experience of God on earth
must come as individual consciousness.

Becoming Free of the Body

Most of you are at the place where there is a "you," a
human being, but now consciously aware of an indwelling
Presence, the Christ or son of God, which is your real identity, even though there is still a part of you not yet experiencing It fully. You are acknowledging that God has incarnated
Himself in you as the Son of God. God, the Father, and
God, the Son, are one, and now God, the Father, is appearing on earth as God, the Son, which you are. That is your
inner spiritual identity and integrity and the source of your
life, your abundance and your happy relationships. As long as
you draw on It and not on people out here, It will manifest.

If you abide in this state of consciousness, eventually
an experience comes that has come to those who are called
mystics. It is an experience, usually in meditation, where suddenly the Spirit is in full play, and for a moment, a minute, or
an hour, you may lose the awareness of your human identity.
You may also become so conscious of yourself as Spirit that
you lose the awareness of your material form. That happens;
there is nothing unusual about it. It happens to students

every week of the year, sometimes every day of the week. It cannot be induced, so please do not try to make it happen because you cannot. You would only defeat your purpose.

It is one of those things that comes by Grace, and it happens in some moment when you are absent from the body, that is, unaware of the physical universe. You are in a state of consciousness where you are free of problems, and that oneness with God can be so acute that you have no sense of your body at all. Then the feeling is that you are out of your body. Sometimes you can look back and see your body, but this is not something that can be induced; it is not something that you can take lessons to attain.

It is something that comes "in such an hour as ye think not,"[15] in a moment when you are not mentalizing, when you are not trying to be something other than you are, when you are just realizing, "Oh, thank God, I am what I am, and I am not going to try to be anything other than what I am. I am not going to try to be spiritual; I am not going to try to be the Christ; I am just satisfied I am what I am." Then it is very likely that you can have an intense spiritual experience, sometimes to the degree of witnessing yourself free of the body.

I and my Father being one, and my Father being Spirit, I am spiritual; and therefore my body is spiritual, and my body is the temple of God.

What you see with your eyes is not your body, but a universal material concept. There is nothing personal about life; it is impersonal. So it is that on the human plane you are not seeing your concept of body: you are seeing the universal concept of body which is the material sense of body. That is what you see with your eyes. If you were to look out at a person with your eyes, you would see his physical form, but what you would really see is the universal concept of him. This is the illusion, because what you see with the eyes is not what is there. What is there is the perfect spiritual temple of God, and it is there that he is tabernacling.

You never lose your physical body because you do not have one: you lose your material concept of body, and then you see face to face. When you look in the mirror, you are seeing "through a glass darkly." When your eyes are closed and you are high in spiritual consciousness, you are seeing face to face. You are seeing a person as he is, and you will be perfectly satisfied with that likeness: "I shall be satisfied, when I awake, with thy likeness,"[16] but you do not see the spiritual form with your eyes. Even if someone who has departed should walk into this room in his ghostlike body, you would still not be seeing his spiritual form: you would be seeing a material concept, because the ghostly body is just as much a material concept as the material body.

It is only when you come to incorporeality, that which is invisible to the eyesight, that you really come to the spiritual temple, a "house not made with hands, eternal in the heavens."[17] This is the body which is your indestructible, immortal, and eternal body. You do not see it and never will see it with your eyes, but every busy practitioner I have ever known has at least once in his life beheld the spiritual body. For most practitioners who have gone far in spiritual understanding, it is not an uncommon experience to behold spiritual creation, not only as the body of a person, but the body of a tree, the body of an ocean, or the body of the sky. What we behold as nature is also not the world of God's creating. That is a universal concept of a star-body, a moon-body, a sun-body, or a tree-body. The reality is incorporeal, invisible, and discernible only to what is called the fourth-dimensional or Christ-consciousness.

I do not believe that anyone has ever remained in the fourth-dimensional consciousness while on earth, although it may be. Certainly I know of no record of it. Almost everyone who has had some measure of spiritual illumination catches a glimpse of reality once in a while, and the higher the individual goes in consciousness, the more apt he is to discern the spiritual body, and at frequent intervals. It is for this reason that the Master went away for forty days and forty nights, so that he could be lifted up in consciousness above the appearance.

The ascension is nothing more nor less than rising above the material, visible concepts into the invisible reality. That is really the significance of the story of Elijah and Elisha. Elisha wanted to be a priest and wear the mantle of the priest, wear Elijah's robe. Elijah's response was, "If thou see me when I am taken from thee, it shall be so unto thee."[18] That is true of all of us. In the moment that we can behold the incorporeal Christ, in that moment the robe of Christhood has fallen upon us. We are now brother or sister to the Christ.

Do not try to accomplish this mentally. You will only fool yourself. It comes by Grace. When Peter saw the Christ appearing as Jesus and said, "Thou art the Christ, the Son of the living God,"[19] the Master answered, "'Flesh and blood hath not revealed it unto thee.'[20] You did not learn this through the five physical senses: my Father within you revealed it to you. Spiritual discernment revealed my Christhood to you." From then on, Peter was a more valuable and probably a more highly honored disciple, although this did not prevent him from falling down in the emergency.

Spiritual Discernment

The ability to behold the Christhood of an individual bears witness to the fact that some measure of spiritual discernment has arisen in you. You can tell by the degree in which you no longer judge, criticize, or condemn, and by the degree in which you can forgive. If it is difficult for you to forgive, if you are still in the stage of being unable to realize, "Father, forgive them; for they know not what they do,"[21] if you are still bearing resentment or desiring revenge, you have not yet attained spiritual discernment. When you attain spiritual discernment, you will know that regardless of what mistake anyone makes, he is making it out of an ignorance of truth and in no other way.

With spiritual discernment you can easily see that the world is the victim of a mass hypnotism based on "self-preservation is the first law of nature." Nothing touches that statement in selfishness because all it says is: "I am out for me, and who cares about you? To save my life, I will take your life; to save my fortune, I will take your fortune. I will get mine, even at the expense of yours." That is a degraded state of consciousness, a mortal and human state of consciousness.

But with the first touch of spiritual discernment, you can understand what the Master meant when he cautioned against an eye for an eye and a tooth for a tooth, against wanting your enemy to be punished. The Master taught his followers to pray for the enemy and forgive him. When you have reached this state of consciousness, you have attained spiritual discernment.

All those who heal spiritually are of that same consciousness. As a human being you would look at a person with a fever, consumption, or paralysis, and you would see what everybody else sees. You would say, "Well, there is nothing we can do about this except what the medical books say." But then as a spiritual practitioner, you say, "No, Christ is the only being. Christ is our only true identity." You rest in that and then afterwards see it fulfilled. How can you look at pneumonia and all the rest of the ills of the flesh without fear when the other person is busily rushing around taking protective serums and doing one thing or another about it? Only because of a developed inner consciousness that has already risen in a degree above the evidence of the senses.

Those who saw the risen Christ were seeing that which is invisible. Just as we have human faculties—the five physical senses—so there are spiritual faculties, soul faculties, an inner awareness that discerns what cannot be humanly known. After the resurrection, there was no physical, visible Jesus walking on earth or everyone would have seen him, but there was the risen Christ. There was that which was raised from the tomb, but which only those of spiritual vision could discern. Only they could discern the man who is never born and the man who will never die.

Your studying and reading reveal things that are antagonistic to the human mind and which the human mind has no way of knowing or recognizing. How then are you going to know them unless you also have that developed, or, in the case of some few, that natural inner intuitional faculty? The development of that faculty comes primarily through meditation. Many persons have been studying metaphysical writings for years and have not even had a tiny glimpse of spiritual vision. They read with the mind, and at no point does intuition reveal what is written between the lines.

As you stand in the presence of sin, disease, lack, limitation, fear, infection, or contagion, you do not surround yourself by might or by power but just by silence. If it becomes a deep enough silence, the entire visible picture will change, and it does through the inner ability to discern that which human-kind never will. You will never perceive the things of God unless you develop Soul-consciousness in a degree, bring forth the inner vision that can see what is invisible, hear what is inaudible, and know what is unknowable. It is with your inner faculties that you discern truth where appearances seem to be.

Sometimes when you are in the depths of meditation, completely absent from this sense of the body, there is the vision of reality, and that encompasses the reality of heaven and earth. Then you begin to perceive that which is the reality of your being and the reality of your body and you can understand why being is not only immortal, but body is immortal.

ACROSS THE DESK

Easter is perhaps the most sacred of all religious holidays. It comes at a time of the rebirth and renewal of all nature, thus signifying the ever-renewing and resurrecting power of the Spirit. Whenever we feel that quickening of the Spirit into newness of life, we, too, have our Easter. It may not come on the day designated as Easter Sunday but when it comes, it will be a resurrection above material sense.

For us, Easter is not a day marked off on the calendar. It is an experience in consciousness. Joy to you as the real Easter is yours.

❖ 5 ❖

JUDGE NOT ACCORDING TO
THE APPEARANCE

GOD IS THE creative principle of the universe. But could there be a God without a universe to which He could be a principle or a law? God is not an unexpressed God. God and Its infinite individuality exist and express simultaneously and instantaneously. I know of no other words to use to bring out the truth that I cannot exist except as I express. Take away expression and what do you have as I? Nothing.

Has there ever been a time when there was a principle of mathematics but no 1, 2, 3, 4, 5, 6, 7, 8, 9, 0? Did the principle of mathematics suddenly decide to appear as 1, 2, 3, 4, 5, 6, 7, 8, 9, 0? Or are the principles of mathematics and its number values simultaneous and instantaneous? Is there a principle of music without do, re, mi, fa, so, la, ti, do or its equivalent in tone? Could there be a principle of music without musical values? If your answer is "Yes," there must have been a principle of music without anything to which it could be a principle. The principle of music is what sustains do, re, mi, fa, so, la, ti, do in their natural values, just as the principle of mathematics sustains to eternity the values of 1, 2, 3, 4, 5, 6, 7, 8, 9, 0. But what would the principle of mathematics or music do without numbers and notes?

Consciousness Is Conscious Of

There is much misleading teaching today on the point that you and I do not exist, that only God exists. How

75

could that possibly be true? Behind what I am saying is the consciousness that exists as the consciousness of that which exists. Consciousness does not exist as a blank. Consciousness exists conscious *of.* It could not be consciousness unless it were conscious *of.* This may sound like an intellectual analysis, but behind it is an intuitive knowledge that there is no awareness without something of which to be aware.

Just as mathematics has its numbers and music its notes, so this principle of Life, which is also the principle of mathematics and music, has Its infinite form and expression, although what we behold on earth is not that.

God as Infinite Individuality

Human society has evolved from the animal state, from the state of a man dragging a woman by the hair into his tent with a "You're mine," to the state where woman has presumably attained equality with man. That is all human unfoldment and evolution; it has nothing to do with God's infinite individuality expressing as individual being. The human state is the prodigal experience which does not testify to infinite individuality.

We do not perceive infinite individuality with our senses. With our senses we see mortals struggling through life from birth to the grave, animals walking around sometimes in human form. The infinite individuality of individual being cannot be seen by looking at a human form, but only by the spiritual discernment that comes in meditation. Then is when we behold God in Its infinite individuality. With our senses we see only the concepts of that individuality and the progressively higher steps of that fallen man or prodigal son on his way back to the Father's house.

Some of us have just left the banquet with the swine, and some have gone a short distance back to the Father's house. Few of us have come to the place where the Father has invested us with that royal ring and robe. When that moment comes we will no longer behold mortality. In our present state of consciousness we are witnessing not so much God's glory in its infinite individuality as mortality in various states of its unfoldment, and higher states of it as we go further along the path back to the Father's household.

Through Inner Vision
Individuality Is Perceived

With inner vision we begin to perceive God in infinite individuality just as Peter discerned It in Jesus when he beheld Jesus as the Christ, or as the three disciples on the Mount of Transfiguration witnessed some degree of the infinite individuality even of those who seemed to have passed from sight hundreds of years before. Those who beheld Jesus risen from the tomb were beholding God in one of Its infinite individual spiritual forms, and they were beholding It the only way in which anyone can behold It, through his spiritual senses.

In an art shop in Beverly Hills, where I saw a painting that to me looked very much like tick-tack-toe squares but which bore the title of "Trafalgar Square," I said, "It can't be. I've seen Trafalgar Square." The art dealer's answer was that this had been painted by a renowned artist and represented what he saw as Trafalgar Square. Obviously, the artist and I were seeing two different things. I was seeing Trafalgar Square with my eyes and he was envisioning something behind the outer scene. It may well be that he was seeing

Trafalgar Square in one of the forms of infinite individuality because often a writer, painter, or sculptor envisions life in some form not discernible through human sense.

Everyone who has attained any mystical sense, that is, any sense of the Father within, has done so only because of an ability to hear that which cannot be heard, see that which cannot be seen, and know that which cannot be known. There is an inner wisdom, an inner vision, an inner discernment that enables a person to respond to the spiritual impulse. Persons of spiritual vision are able to behold something that others do not see.

What Is Righteous Judgment?

One of the deepest principles, if not the deepest, necessary both in spiritual living and spiritual healing, is based on a scriptural quotation, "Judge not according to the appearance, but judge righteous judgment."[1] Very often this is interpreted as meaning that we are not to judge evil from appearances, but that it is considered all right to judge good. The statement does not mean that at all. The Master rebuked those who called him "Good Master." "Why callest thou me good? there is none good but one, that is, God."[2] He taught that even to judge that he himself was good was erroneous. So in living this principle, no one has the right to judge good any more than he has the right to judge evil.

By appearances, how can we in any way judge? The healthiest looking person in the world may drop dead of heart disease the next minute. The point is that we are neither well nor sick, neither good nor evil, neither rich nor poor. God is infinite and only God *is*. That leaves out any degree of comparison.

Rising Above the Pairs of Opposites

In all spiritual teaching it is said that we must rise above the pairs of opposites to where there is neither good nor evil, young nor old, alive nor dead, sick nor well, rich nor poor, male nor female, but to where there is only One, and that One is God: infinite, immortal, eternal, harmonious, perfect, joyous, free. That is why The Infinite Way teaches that we never get free from anything, from anybody, or from any condition. In spiritual truth we find our freedom in Christ; we find our freedom in Truth, in Spirit; but never can we find our freedom *from*. Why? Because spiritual freedom is not involved in any thing.

One of the principles that has helped us in our work with human relationships—family, business, capital and labor—is the principle that right is not on the side of capital or labor, on the side of husband or wife, or of parent or child. The only right is God. By standing on that truth, harmony begins to appear wherever there is a degree of receptivity to it. It does not mean that everybody will be healed or made happy. It means that wherever there is a degree of receptivity, being one with God constitutes the majority.

The person judged as good or as moral today may fall from the human standard of goodness or morality at any given moment. There is no use judging him good or moral just because he may conform to some pattern of goodness or morality at a particular moment. The one you have accepted today as well or rich may make a liar out of you tomorrow. By not judging by appearances but holding to the righteous judgment that God is the infinite One, harmony is brought out.

In every instance where we can rise above judging whether the wife or the husband is right, the parent or the child, and hold to the truth that not one of them can be right because God alone is right, then the rightness of God, omnipresent where we are, is revealed. Miracles happen, all by not judging either good or evil.

It has been the experience of every mystic who has attained conscious union with God—even if he attained that conscious union only in moments of meditation—that he rose above all sense of right or wrong, good or bad, male or female, to where there was just a state of being: not being somebody or being some thing, but just being, and being aware of his infinite Being. Sometimes he was being out in the ocean or up in a tree. That sense of omnipresence enabled him to rise above the limited finite sense of self.

In a Healing Contemplative Meditation Release All Judgment

When a practitioner is presented with a problem, whether it is physical, mental, moral, or financial, instinctively and unconsciously there is a desire to correct the wrong and make it right. In other words, if a person's breathing is labored, the desire is to see him breathe properly; if he has a fever, the desire is to reduce his temperature to normal. If he is not having adequate elimination, the desire is to bring about elimination, all for the purpose of changing evil into good. That is not the mode or method of Infinite Way work.

Our work takes no cognizance of what is called human normalcy. We go right through or beyond the appearance and recognize that there is but One good—good in health, good in wealth, good in harmony—and that One is God: God omnipotent, God omnipresent, God the All-in-All. By holding to that, harmony appears in what we call the human picture.

Through steadfastly holding to the truth of God's all-ness—not your goodness, your good health, good wealth, or good morals—and by ignoring the appearance of good and evil, the healing comes about that results in what we call improved humanhood, that is, a sick person becomes well, an unemployed person becomes employed, an immoral person becomes moral.

The moment we come down to judging by appearances, we lose spiritual power. For thousands of years, people have been telling others how bad they are, and then trying to make them better. There is no way spiritually to accomplish that. The Master's secret was: What did hinder you? What power is there to prevent you from taking up your bed and walking? And there is not any, since God is infinite power.

God, the Actor, the Be-er, the Do-er

Over and over in Jesus' teaching he says, "I can of mine own self do nothing. ... If I bear witness of myself, my witness is not true.[3] My doctrine is not mine, but his that sent me."[4] Always his message was a presentation of the great revelation that only God is doing, acting, and being. There is no good "me," and there is no spiritual "me," and there is no "me" as the Savior: there is only God. When we can take the attitude that whatever is coursing through us is God, we will not claim personal good, but in not claiming personal good, we will not claim personal evil either. Here we come to the hardest part.

It is one thing to say of ourselves, "I am neither good nor evil. It is God that works in me. Whatever qualities I have are qualities of God." But how different and how difficult it is when we look out in the world and see some of the evil characters and some of the very good ones! We cannot help loving and admiring the good ones, and we cannot help condemning, criticizing, and judging the evil ones, or at least knowing how they could be better. A line must be drawn in our consciousness that enables us to stop judging the appearance, so that we can look through it and say, "I am not interested if the appearance at the moment is good or evil, whether the fever is up or down, or the pocketbook full or empty. I am looking through to the truth that God alone is. And because God alone is, all is well.

Sacrificing Concepts as a Form of Giving and Purification

In the material sense of life the whole secret is getting. In the spiritual sense of life the whole secret is giving. Many people have misunderstood that principle and thought that it meant to give money to their church or to charity. That is not necessarily giving. It can be, but that is not what giving means. Giving means sharing what is nearest and dearest and closest to us, just as in the case of the Hebrew prophet who was called upon to offer up his son.

And what is the most important thing we have to give up? What, but our concepts of God and man. We have to sacrifice everything we believe about each other; we must be willing to give up some of our most cherished beliefs including the belief that Jesus of himself was good. That is a hard sacrifice. So, too, we must give up the belief that some dictator is bad, that our friends are good and our enemies bad. In short, we have to give up the thing that is hardest for us to give up, and that is our concept of God and man.

Only through sacrifice do we find God. The Hebrews

sacrificed: lambs, doves, and ten percent of their income. But the Master told them that would do no good: "Sacrifice and offering and burnt offerings and offering for sin thou wouldest not, neither hadst pleasure therein."[5] Today many people believe that in giving up their money or some other thing they are pleasing God. There is no way to please God except to give up our judgments of each other, our hates and loves until we come to the place where we can say, "There is but one good, the Father in heaven. God is the soul of every individual." In the prisons? Yes. In Russia? Yes. Black? Yes. White? Yes. Yellow? Yes. Red? Yes. God is the soul of every individual being. See no exceptions to that no matter what you see the person doing. Stand on God as the soul of every individual. Judge not.

The Master did not judge the adulterous woman; he did not judge the thief on the cross; he did not judge the boy born blind or his parents. The Master seldom judged. He never as much as judged himself to be good, not even while he was healing and feeding multitudes. When Peter recognized him as the Christ, he did not give Peter the credit. He said, "Flesh and blood hath not revealed it unto thee, but my Father which is in heaven."[6]

God Alone Is Understanding

Every once in a while someone writes me a letter about how much studying he has done and how great his understanding is, but the demonstration does not come. I write back, "Yes, but you have missed the whole point. You thought you had an understanding. Where did you get it? I thought God alone was the mind of the individual. If that is true, then God alone has understanding, and you have just been absorbing something that you thought was yours. As long as you hold to the fact that you have understanding, you are never going to do healing work, nor are you going to be healed, unless somebody has a greater realization than you have. It is not true that you have understanding, and all that you have ever learned is not going to increase your understanding one little bit."

God alone is good. God alone is the intelligence of this universe, and if there is any understanding, it is the understanding of God. We of our own selves, with all the truth we can learn in all the books, cannot heal a headache. But the power of God, operating in our consciousness, can raise the dead. It is the power of God, not your understanding or my understanding. There is no such thing as your understanding or mine, any more than there is such a thing as *your* goodness or *my* goodness, *your* health or *my* health. Just try to claim health for yourself and see what happens. It is not true. God is the soul of your being. God is the soul of the universe. God is the soul of the animal world, the vegetable world, the mineral world, and as you recognize that fact, that truth will be reflected back to you in your experience.

Righteous Judgment Is Rendered in the Silence

There is only one way to know that this is true. That is when God tells us within our own being, and It tells us only when we are still, when we are silent and listen for that still, small voice. Then the voice utters itself within us, and when the Word comes, It stills the waves, It opens the Red Sea. Moses did not open the Red Sea, and Jesus did not multiply loaves and fishes: they opened their consciousness and let the power of God come through, and the power of God did it. When Moses opened his mouth, he was told that God would put the words on his lips. Jesus recognized, "I can of mine own self do nothing."

So it is with you and with me. I open my mouth, have an inner listening ear, and the words come rolling out. God has to put them there because if God does not put them there, they are not going to register with you. They would just be my words to you, and such words would be without power. Only as the word of God flows through can you say or feel, "This is truth. This is it. This is the revelation of God." Then we become instruments in this ministry.

Whether we are artists, painters, sculptors, or musicians, we are all instruments for the divine consciousness to flow through, instruments for Its use. Every individual, whether he writes music or poetry, builds bridges or houses, whatever he does, should do it for the purpose of showing forth God's glory. When he does not realize that his function is to show forth God's glory, his abilities become limited and finite because he is depending only on his education and ability.

Becoming Established
in the Rhythm of God

As we come more and more into the realization of our spiritual individuality, there is a certain groove or rhythm in consciousness into which we individually fit, and when so established we find ourselves in outer circumstances, places, or conditions of peace and harmony. This peace is not a static peace; at times it is a vital state of spiritual being and activity; at times it is a deep stillness and quiet within and a joy in worldly affairs.

Becoming established in the rhythm of God may appear as warfare since "I came not to send peace, but a sword."[7] This warfare represents a surrender of self, sometimes a painful one, before the realization of spiritual harmony and spiritual selfhood is attained. It is the laying off of the cocoon as the butterfly unfolds. In meditation and in quiet contemplation of the Soul, we achieve a spiritual rhythm and only then know the government and the realm of Spirit. Established in the rhythm of life, we rest in the Soul, find recompense and activity in the new dimension, Christ. Our values are no longer based on material estimates, but rather are measured by the standards of "My kingdom," which is love.

Grace Becomes Active in Our Experience When Consciousness Is Purified

Good in our experience is the direct result of our being in the consciousness of good. Our consciousness must be purged of its false concepts of God and of individual being which we call man. In giving up our false concepts of man and our false sense of being, our consciousness is pure and clear, ready to be receptive and responsive to good.

To resist not evil is also a purification of consciousness, since it is separating ourselves from the belief of a power and a presence other than good. Once consciousness is cleared of the belief of a selfhood apart from God or an activity, substance, or law apart from God, consciousness is then ready for the blessing of divine Grace.

Grace is not something that is given to us or withheld from us. Grace is a state of being which comes into active expression the moment consciousness has been purified, just as the law of gravity comes into operation when an object is

dropped. The law of gravity is always present and in operation, but nothing happens until an object is released. Divine
Grace is forever present in our consciousness, but It cannot
operate, that is, It cannot manifest or express in the presence of the barrier of fear or hate. It cannot exist side by side
with the belief of a selfhood apart from God or an activity,
substance, or law apart from good.

When consciousness is freed of erroneous beliefs and
concepts, then we are prepared to commune with God, to
rest in the Soul, and to be at peace. There is really nothing
that can disturb an individual who neither hates, fears, nor
loves the objects of sense. Where there is no attempt at any
time or in any way to gain something from God and when
we are free of judgments, prayer is a resting in the Soul, a
state of receptivity. It is that and more, because it brings
peace and a sense of satisfaction in pure being. There, not
even expectancy arises. There is only the satisfaction and the
sense of completeness in God which is the ultimate of prayer.
There is nothing to be desired, nothing to be attained, not
even protection, safety, or security. There is then and forever
a sense of perfection attained, of pure rest in the Soul.

ACROSS THE DESK

By this time, you have had an opportunity to explore
Living Between Two Worlds[8] and must have discovered its
rich treasures, and for each of you it holds its special treasure.

In conjunction with your study of the important lesson
in this month's letter, the chapter, "Making the Transition
from Personal Sense to Spiritual Being," in the new book,
will be especially significant to you. Let me share just a brief
excerpt with you:

"When you make the transition to the man who lives 'by every word that proceedeth out of the mouth of God,' you form no judgments, but rather create a vacuum within yourself, resulting in an attitude of listening so that divine judgment can be rendered. Then you will discover that you never hear or see good or evil, but rather that the man and the universe of God's creating are revealed to you, and you see the people about whom you had entertained judgments of one kind or another in an entirely different light."

I heartily commend the whole chapter to you as an aid in gaining a deeper awareness of how to attain the consciousness of no judgment of a person or a condition as to whether it is good or evil, but letting inner discernment reveal spiritual identity and spiritual perfection and wholeness.

TAPE RECORDED EXCERPTS
Prepared by the Editor

Do we have to accept the mesmerism of lack and limitation as a fact of life in this day and age or must we, as Infinite Way students, "come out and be separate," recognizing only the omnipresence of all good? Is there an answer? Yes, and here it is:

The Silver Is Mine

"Acknowledge that the silver is the Lord's and the gold is the Lord's, and the power is the Lord's. Now begin to understand 'the earth is the Lord's, and the fullness thereof,' and 'Son,... all that I have is thine.' Now you are not... dividing up what is out in the world. Now *I* within you is multiplying out of the unseen resources of Spirit, not drawing upon the visible resources of the earth, but now drawing forth from the invisible storehouse within your own being. Now it is multiplied from within you.

"The moment you acknowledge, 'The earth is the Lord's, and the fullness thereof,' the silver is God's and the gold is God's, then you have really given up possession of the things of the outer world, and acknowledged the fullness of the inner world. Then it begins to flow, whether it flows as the multiplication of loaves and fishes or the multiplication of oil in the cruse or ravens bringing food. From the moment you say, "The silver is the Lord's, the gold is the Lord's, the earth and all the fullness thereof belongs to God, and 'Son, ... all that I have is thine,'" you begin to draw from an infinite storehouse within your own being that never has to count what is out here in the visible world. It never has to be concerned with how much or how little. Whether there is a boom on or whether there is a depression going on, that has nothing to do with you; it will not come nigh your dwelling. Neither the boom nor the depression will come nigh your dwelling place because you now will have recognized that the silver is God's and the gold is God's.

"'The earth is the Lord's, and the fullness thereof,' and that is all I care about because if I know that... I'm sure I'll have all I need every day. It is only when I believe that the earth and the silver and the gold [and the oil] belong to you and how am I going to get some of it [that I am concerned]. That has been the error: the silver and the gold and the earth are all out here belonging to the land barons and the money barons, and how are we going to be clever enough to get some of it away from them. They have twice as many brains holding on to it as we have going out to get it. They even have big law firms to help them hold on to it, and here we go out all alone to try to squeeze some of it out of them. It can't be done. But... you have to continue realizing: 'The earth is the Lord's.'

"God neither gives nor withholds, and therefore, man has no power to give or withhold. Everything comes to us by the grace of God, and as we learn that, we learn that the storehouse is within our own being. ... God has given to us infinite bounty, and it is unlimited when we recognize that. ... God is infinite in being and infinite in expression, and this infinity of God is pouring through me to you as truth. ... And so it is with our supply of daily food, clothing, housing, currency, [and oil]. The only thing is to be sure that we are looking to our Source for it, not to each other."

Joel S. Goldsmith, "Except the Lord, Psalm 127,"
The 1954 Chicago Practitioners' Class.

"Infinite good is already established within your own consciousness, and you are not going to add good to yourself. You are going to learn through practice to let your good flow out from within your own being. God is the law operating in and as your own consciousness, and because God is infinite, your consciousness is infinite. Therefore, your consciousness... includes now the substance of everything necessary to your experience unto eternity—if you live seven billion years, which you will. The substance of all that is necessary for your unfoldment is at this very moment embodied within you, ... ready to appear in natural unfoldment. ... The completeness and perfection of your life is already established within you as essence or substance, and it appears outwardly as form. Your part is to learn to sit back, to have your moment of meditation: *The Invisible, the invisible substance of my being, the invisible consciousness, the invisible soul of me is the essence of all form.*"

Joel S. Goldsmith, "Transcendental,"
The 1952 Honolulu Closed Class.

"In the height of the depression, the President said that forty percent of the population was undernourished. Was that because there was not enough food in existence or because man was destroying the food? The food was there. The seas never ran short of fish; the air never ran short of birds; Maine never ran short of potatoes; the Midwest never ran short of wheat;

the South never ran short of cotton. The infinity of supply has been eternal even when men were starving to death for lack of it.

"The only lack there is in this world is love in the hearts of man. That is all. There is no lack of God's grace. There is no lack of God's abundance. God has not punished mankind by withholding food and articles of clothing. God has not punished mankind for his sins. The earth is full of the riches of God. The skies declare the glory and the earth shows forth the handiwork of God, and believe me it is beautiful and it is abundant and infinite. ... The moment we let that love flow through us, that love appears tangibly in our experience as the health and wealth of body and purse."

Joel S. Goldsmith, "Principles of Spiritual Living,"
The 1954 Third New York Practitioners' Class.

❖ 6 ❖

THE MIDDLE PATH

MOST PERSONS ARE praying to God and turning to the Christ to have their nets filled with fish instead of following the Master's teaching to leave their nets. Leave all! Do not seek companionship; seek *My* companionship and see what happens. There is a new dimension, another plane of consciousness, in which a person does not seek human good, human companionship, or human supply, in which he does not seek anything of a human nature. Rather he seeks to forsake his dependence on things as well as his dependence on mother, father, sister, or brother. Then he gains the spiritual sense of parenthood, childhood, husbandhood, wifehood, and spiritual wholeness.

Spiritual Regeneration Is
the Goal of Infinite Way Work

Let us assume that someone who is ill has asked for help. With that call for help, you are being presented with a human being, at the moment ill and aging. Even if he is only sixteen years of age, he is aging. In traditional metaphysical practice the idea is to make this person well. If he tells you that he has a temperature of 104 degrees, and calls up later to say that it has gone down to 102, you breathe a sigh of relief and say, "Isn't that fine?" An hour later he calls and tells you that it is 98.6. Ah, that's perfect!

The next person may call because he has burned himself and is in pain, but when an hour later there is not even a scar where the burn was, again comes that sigh of relief. The call may come that another person is dying, and the doctor's prognosis is that he will be gone in three hours, but three hours after the call for help the patient is sitting up, drinking orange juice. Again comes that sense of "How wonderful!" That is all based on the fact that John Jones was dying, but now he is alive. As a matter of fact he may be so alive that he goes to work the next day and is run over by a trolley car. In the early years of my practice I had two experiences similar to that.

After years of being under a doctor's care, a man dying of heart disease was told that the last attack gave him no further hope of coming through the experience. He agreed that his wife should ask for spiritual help, and five weeks later a cardiograph showed no scar on his heart, not a trace of heart disease, and never again did he have a single murmur from his heart.

The man decided that now that he was so well he would devote himself to making money, which he succeeded in doing. Two years later, however, he committed suicide. Life had become utterly unendurable to him. His heart was not bothering him but something else was. The healing had not brought spiritual regeneration, nor any desire for God. Nothing more had happened than that a sick man had been made well. It had not added any desire for life to him or given him anything of permanent value since outer success or money can be only transitory happiness unless it is incidental to something greater than itself.

There was another case of a man dying of leukemia. One of our students met his wife and when told how seriously ill the man was, the student suggested spiritual help. When the patient said he did not believe in such nonsense, the student came to me disturbed and asked, "Do we have to accept that verdict?"

My response was, "Aren't you forgetting the teaching of The Infinite Way? What verdict? What man? What have we to do with a sick man? Are we in the business of healing sick people? Are we primarily concerned with whether a person is sick or well? We are not doctors. We have nothing to do with prolonging a person's life. Our work is the realization of God as individual identity. Is God any less this man's identity whether he is to our sense living or dead, sick or well?

A few days later the man was released from the hospital completely healed. A miracle had taken place that the doctors said they had never seen, but which certainly sometimes happens. When the patient was released from the hospital, the student went to him and told him about this experience. His response was, "Nonsense. The doctors said those things happen every once in a while." He decided that since a second chance had been given him, he would build a beautiful home for his wife. He began building immediately, and one day when he was inspecting the roof he fell off and was killed.

Again there had been no spiritual regeneration; there was no turning from material sense to Spirit. Evidently for one reason or another, both of these men had come to the end of their span and there was nothing that could be done to prolong it. Both had the opportunity, had they been prepared for it, for some kind of a spiritual awakening to their true identity, which might have changed the whole course of their human experience.

Not Good Health or
Bad Health but Christhood

Are we interested in whether a person's tombstone has inscribed on it 1953 or 1985? Except for some human reason, is it important what date is on that tombstone? Is not our work the realization of the Christ as individual life, never born and never dying? Is not that our vision? So even when we see a room full of healthy people, the realization must come that Christ is their true identity. Our recognition must go beyond sickness or wellness, aliveness or deadness because, alive or dead, Christ is their true identity, even if they cannot accept it.

What happens to you in the moment when a person turns to you for help is the secret of healing work. Are you going to try to improve him, or are you going to sit there in the realization of Christhood? That is the crux of the matter. The moment you enter into human sympathy with a person, have a desire to heal, improve, reform, or correct him, you are working from the basis of human regeneration, and when you have completed your work, you will still have a human being. That is not your function.

The work of Infinite Way students is the realization of Christhood, the revelation of God individualized no matter who or what a person may be. The Master could take the thief on the cross into paradise immediately. He had no period of punishment, reformation, or regeneration to go through; he had no karma to work out.

"Though your sins be as scarlet, they shall be as white as snow."[1] When? When you turn to the recognition of your Christhood. But you say that you may sin again tomorrow. That has nothing to do with it. You may sin tomorrow and the day after and next week, too. What counts is that you have turned to the realization of your Christhood.

If you are led to someone who has enough light in him to bring forth your Christhood, It will come. Whether the realization comes instantaneously as in some cases or whether it is the slow process of moving out of material consciousness into spiritual consciousness makes no difference. It might have been far better if the two men cited above had not had instantaneous healings. It might have been better if they had been compelled to dig in and work until they came to some measure of realization than to have had instantaneous healings that as far as they were concerned were just physical disease becoming physical health.

I call this way the Middle Path. When you set forth on it, you begin to attain the inner faculty that enables you, when a call comes, to disregard the human being with all his ails and ills, and remember, "Wait a minute. What am I doing? What is my mission? There is only one Son of God and that is the Christ. I have nothing to do with the infinite forms and varieties as which It appears. There is but one Son of God, the Christ, and It was never born and It will never die. It was immaculately conceived. It is God unfolding, disclosing, and revealing Itself in infinite form and variety without any human accompaniment, without any human mode or means, and always perfect, spiritual, and harmonious."

Spiritual Identity,
Not Human Birth or Death

A case was brought to me of a breech birth. When the telephone rang, there was only one vision that I had: it was not of a mother having a baby because there wasn't anything that I could do about that. It was the fact of spiritual identity. The Christ is the only being and It was never conceived, It was never born, and It will never die. There is only one being and that is the Christ. I was in the Middle Path where there is not a mother giving birth, where there are no mothers, not even spiritual mothers: only the Christ in Its full-blown identity. With that vision the baby turned around and brought itself forth.

If you look at it from the standpoint of a possibly fatal delivery turned into a satisfactory one, you miss the point entirely. There can be no human intervention, not even mentally. In this case there was not even the recognition or declaration that it is the Christ that does the work. It was some inner faculty that enabled me to know that we are not mortals going through an experience of birth and death.

Indifference to Humanhood

The moment your thought goes to your patient in any human way to give advice as to whether he should have a change of climate, whether he should sleep with the windows open or closed, or whether he should change his food, you are out of the Middle Path. You are really out of spiritual healing and back in mental, dietetic, or physical healing. We have nothing to do with an individual's diet. He will be divinely led to eat and drink the right things. If his food is of such poor quality that is it not giving him proper nourishment, he may even be divinely led to take vitamins. There is nothing wrong about that because vitamins are only food in another form.

You, however, will have no part in that except your recognition of the Middle Path: the Christ as true being. You may have patients ask, "Shall I give up smoking? Shall I give up drinking?" From the standpoint of healing, you are not interested in making them better human beings, not a bit. You do not care if they smoke or drink or jump off the roof. All you are interested in is recognizing the Christ of their being. Your constant recognition of that Christhood results in Christ revealing, manifesting, and expressing Itself. A statement of truth will not make it so.

You must come to a place in the Middle Path of a kind of indifference to humanhood. You lose all desire to heal; you lose all desire to reform. But a wonderful thing happens. You lose all criticism of people who are living up to your human standards of what is right or wrong. You no longer differentiate between saint and sinner; you no longer differentiate between the good human being and the bad human being because into your vision comes the realization of true identity.

Everyone will awaken to his Christhood—some instantaneously, some quickly, some slowly, and some interminably slowly. It involves a transition within them from the material sense of existence to the spiritual. It entails the dropping away of human characteristics, human faults, human failings until they themselves enter the spiritual realm of existence. It may for a while involve training yourself to utter indifference to the human picture while you stand on spiritual integrity, on the Christhood of the individual. That means that as the temptation comes to you to believe that you have some sickness to overcome you will be consciously realizing, "I am not using God as a power to do something; I am not turning to God for a miracle: I am standing fast in the realization that in spiritual living we need no miracles; in spiritual living harmony already is."

Being Is, Not Becoming

It is not too difficult to be on the Middle Path if you have the help of the word *is*, because if you are tempted to do something to improve the human scene, you can come back to *is*. *Is*, is the only truth, *is*, is. As you hold to *is*, you lose the temptation to try to change the human picture.

Certain philosophies teach that being is becoming. Being cannot be becoming: being is. True, it may be coming to your awareness, just as the young child each day learns something about the world and to its sense it is as if it were becoming so, but to yours it has always been that way. The child is merely becoming aware of that which is. So spiritually you may be learning new truths each day, or thinking you are, but actually you are becoming aware of what is.

Healing works consists in the recognition of the Christhood of individual being which already is. You do not need any God or God-power to make It so. All that is needed is your vision to behold Christhood. Never attempt to bring It about either by healing or reforming.

Freedom in Christ

Stand fast in the Middle Path with the realization of Christhood and let the good human being and the bad human being be what he is at any given moment. Let the sick or the well human being be whatever he is. Do not feel elated about 98.6 temperature because it can change from down to up in a second. You have no temperature: you have only Christhood. Do not be elated about the lump going down and do not be alarmed about the lump going up. You have nothing to do with lumps: you have to do with Christhood.

Your vision is not the changing of physical conditions: your vision is the vision of eternal infinite Christhood. It is not a vision of your healing someone of something or making him into something else. Christhood is the established and permanent identity. Jesus revealed It; Mrs. Eddy revealed It; later Unity revealed It; and The Infinite Way is revealing It.

At this particular stage, however, Infinite Way work has gone another step in that it is not interested in changing humanhood. We have now come to the point of the Master's revelation where he says, "My kingdom is not of this world.[2]... Who made me a judge or a divider over you?"[3] He was not going to raise up an army to free the Hebrews either from Rome or the Hebrew Church. They could stay in that slavery as long as they clung to their human identity. He may have thought that this slavery would wake them up and bring them to the realization of their Christhood sooner, and then they would not be in bondage to any man or any government, to any physical, mental, moral, or economic condition. No person can be freed from error: he can be freed only in Christ.

When a person is free in Christ, he is not freed from anything. No one can free a person from an unhappy marriage, a frustrating or unrewarding job, or a failing business. When you can reveal his spiritual freedom in Christ, however, that will break all material, mental, moral, and economic fetters. No one can free a person from a sick and ailing body. It is the realization of the Christ that sets a person free. Nothing really changes except his concept of body which continuously changes until all concepts have been given up through working with the idea of *is*.

Body Is, but What Is It?

Some day you will work with the idea of *is*, and then you will put no labels on anything. For example, think of the word *body* and acknowledge that there is only one thing you really know about body: body is. You are aware of your body so you know that it is. Anything beyond that at this present moment is a concept. It may be your concept of body or it may be a concept that you have accepted through universal belief, a concept handed down to you through racial, religious, or national beliefs, so you entertain that concept of body. But you really know nothing about body at this minute, so you can acknowledge, "Yes, body is, but what is body?" That sets up a question which creates a vacuum, a state of receptivity. From there on, spiritual sense must define to you what body is.

That definition must come from within. You must be taught of God, not of man. Therefore, you do not want anybody's concept of or thought about body. Body is, but what is it? With that question your ear of receptivity is open. There is an inner vacuum waiting to be filled. As you practice that form of meditation, eventually you will catch a vision of the nature of body.

Let Spirit Define Itself

With every subject that comes to your attention, you can begin with the idea that you know nothing about it except that it is. It *is*. What is it? As you meditate from the standpoint of *is*, the Spirit within begins to define what is. When you are called upon for help, do not think or declare that it is not true or that it is not real. In other words, do not try to negate it. Instead, come into agreement with it and acknowledge that something has come to your awareness. Something is. The only thing you do not know about it is what it is. The world may say it is evil, but you know it cannot be evil because God is the only creative principle. Why deny something that cannot be evil? It makes no difference what its name or nature is because actually you do not know its name or nature or what it is.

Something has touched consciousness. You do not know what it is and you are going to put no labels on it: no judgment, criticism, or condemnation, and no praise. Metaphysicians become aware of evil and then turn around and call the evil, spiritual being. They see an inebriate who is unable to stand on his feet and say, "you are a spiritual being. You are the Christ." They see somebody dying of disease or poverty and call that spiritual.

I see more clearly now, not that we must deny it, but that we must agree with our adversary and not resist evil. Resisting evil is the acknowledgment of evil. "Thou shalt have no other gods before me."[4] Thou shalt not acknowledge any other creative principle or sustaining power. Do not take up the sword of denial but rather see what happens when you take the opposite standpoint of *is*. To say that it is not evil but spiritual is still putting a label on it, making a judgment of it. When you call a thing good, that represents your concept of it, and somebody else has the right to claim that this very same thing is evil or wrong. The moment you say it is good, someone else may say it is bad. Regardless of what concept you may hold, you, yourself, may at the next moment change that concept.

When you begin to work from the standpoint of *is*, something very wonderful happens within you. Begin this very day with any of the things that require attention—whether in your own experience or that of another—and work from the standpoint of *is*. You do not know what a particular thing is, so with the inner ear open, let Spirit define to you what it is. It will be revealed that whatever of evil was there was not there as evil but as an appearance that has now disappeared through not fighting it.

A rope presenting the illusion of a snake will never disappear while you are denying it and claiming it is evil and certainly it will not disappear while you are saying it is spiritual. There is only one way in which the snake will disappear and that is by your realization that something is presenting itself to you, and then letting your inner vision reveal that it is rope not snake. In the case of illness where the "snake" you are seeing is a disease but you do not know what the "rope" of wholeness is, watch what happens as you look at this from the standpoint of *is* and let the inner light define it for you.

Place No Labels on Anyone or Anything

Be very careful not to label a person as being good or bad, rich or poor, up or down, saint or sinner. Put no labels on Jones, Brown, or Smith. Do not judge after appearances. When some person comes into your consciousness, withdraw your judgment or the world's judgment or opinion of him, and agree on *is:* "Something or someone is touching my consciousness. Now Father, what?" This will bring about an entirely different relationship with people, even with those who would injure you if they could but cannot injure you because they do not have that power.

With those who despitefully use you, gossip, or slander, watch the difference in your reaction to them as you do not grasp at the straw of appearances and try to hold onto it. Look at them without any desire to change them. Have only the desire to hold them as they are in truth, and that is something you cannot do with your mind. You could accept somebody's word that everyone is the Christ of God, but repeating that or making statements about it will not demonstrate it or do much for you. You will bring it out only by not judging by appearances.

Where is this principle leading you? Not merely to the point of healing disease, sin, or lack. No, you must come to the place of looking at the healthiest or wealthiest human being you know, withdraw your concepts, and stop judging after appearances. Neither picture is true.

Good humanhood can become bad humanhood; alive humanhood can become dead humanhood; rich humanhood can become poor humanhood; saintly humanhood can become sinful humanhood. So even when you are looking at a very beautiful human picture, even when you yourself are enjoying good health and supply, do not believe it. Turn within in the realization that something is, and let the spiritual truth of being reveal itself to you. The moment your heart, liver, or lungs, and your weekly income or lack of it do not bother you, you are more than likely enjoying the health of your body or the wealth of your pocketbook and you may be opening yourself to a sudden change.

Treatment or Meditation as Receptivity

It becomes necessary for us to use this teaching of *Is* even with good appearances, even with good humanhood. Having done that, whatever flows to you as health or wealth becomes no longer good health or material wealth by chance but the outpouring of the spiritual realization or spiritual awareness of health and wealth. That is an entirely different story. You do not judge by appearances even when it is a good appearance. You look through the appearance to *is* and then behold spiritual entity and spiritual identity.

In approaching any problem from this standpoint you are increasing the effectiveness of your treatment or meditation. In metaphysics, as usually taught, treatment is denial. In The Infinite Way meditation is the realization of *is*. Now you are right in the midst of your treatment or meditation which is a state of receptivity, a listening for that inner unfoldment, not for the treatment which *you* are going to give, but for the treatment which God is going to give. The treatment is given within you. God does the praying.

Had I not known for many years that no mental activity of mind would heal anybody, I would not be standing on the Master's great principle of "I can of mine own self do nothing."[5] If any mental activity of mine or any thought of mine could heal anybody, it would be ludicrous to say I am not doing it. The truth is that I cannot heal and I do not know any truth that will heal. You could take all the books of The Infinite Way and recite them from cover to cover and you would not heal anything. There must be a prayer from within which is the word of God coming to human consciousness.

"For the word of God is quick, and powerful, and sharper than any two-edged sword.[6]... It shall not return unto me void."[7] How many times have you meditated and watched the meditation return void? How many treatments have you given that have not been productive of results? They were not the word of God: they were your words, the words you read in a book. They were man's words, man's concept of truth.

The word of God is an impulse that you receive in your ear within your own being. It may come as a quotation, an assurance, a feeling, or it may come just as a sense of release, but it is the word of God, the presence of God made flesh in you. When that word of God comes, be assured it does not return void. Whenever you have had an experience of that kind and then have heard later that there was an instantaneous healing, you were not surprised. You knew it must have happened because you could feel when it really was the word of God, not some word repeated out of a book.

Words or Statements Are Relative

Never do you give up treatment, but treatment may eventually come to a place where it takes only one second. If a problem is presented to you, you may quickly realize *is*, and that might be the whole treatment. In that one word is encompassed a whole book. You may remind yourself of *is* and then sit in the silence for five, ten, or twenty minutes, receiving an unfoldment until the moment of complete release comes.

God's allness is the absolute truth. But that Allness reveals Itself to you sometimes in relative ways. The very use of words of truth to lift you into the consciousness of oneness is a relative activity. Once the heavenly state of consciousness is realized, there is no need for words, statements, or reminders of truth. Then people could come to you and sit with you for a minute, an hour, or a week, and walk on healed because you would be in such a high state of being that you would be completely unaware of any discord. That would be the Absolute. The moment you began to talk to students or patients about truth, you would again be in the relative. In the realization of *is*, you cannot think another thought about what is, how it is, or how much is. You have shut yourself up the minute you have said, "Is."

As you live in the attitude of *is*, you never form an opinion about anything or anyone: you wait for Spirit to reveal the true picture. Living in this consciousness, somebody may reach out to you for help. He may write a letter, telephone, or send a telegram, and receive his healing before you are consciously aware that he is reaching out to you. That is healing in the Absolute. He has touched the Absolute of your consciousness, and you humanly have not entered the picture, not even to the extent of saying, *"Is."*

A teacher and lecturer who had been away on a lecture trip found his mail stacked up at his hotel and on top of the pack a cablegram. The cable read, "Thanks for instantaneous healing." The teacher handed the cable to the student who had met him at the airport and said, "You see what a good teacher you have? An instantaneous healing! Now let's see when the healing took place and what it was."

With that, the teacher dug through his mail to find another cable, and there it was, asking for help for an emergency. The teacher had had no conscious knowledge of the need, but living in his high consciousness of truth he had been reached. That was an absolute healing. It was the same type of healing experienced by the woman who pushed through the throng and touched the robe of the Master. Jesus was not consciously aware of her presence; nevertheless she was healed. And he very honestly said, "Daughter, thy faith hath made thee whole; go in peace, and be whole of thy plague."[8] In other words her reaching out had touched the Absolute of his consciousness and without any conscious effort on his part she was healed.

There are persons who write letters to me, and before the letters could have left the mailbox, the healing has come. In other cases people have telephoned and received no answer, and yet a few minutes later their healing took place. These things happen frequently. They are absolute healings, because it is the touching of the Christhood of the practitioner's being in which no human factor enter. Once a person has asked for help, and you respond with *is*, you have entered the picture and, when the release from the Spirit has come, then again you are in the Absolute. But while you are *is-ing* you are in the relative.

I do something about everything and about everybody brought to my consciousness, but not always the same thing. Sometimes it is necessary that I sit for a long time before what I have to do is accomplished. But at other times it may come instantaneously.

Once I have realized the consciousness of the Absolute, then the healing takes place, but first I have to come to the point of realization. That can be called treatment, even if no human thought is involved. It is just a waiting until that beautiful sense of release and of peace comes. That is the attainment of the Absolute, and it is in that attainment that the miracle takes place. You may ask if I gave a treatment or had a healing meditation. Sitting and waiting for the attainment of that Absolute even if I do not have a conscious thought is a treatment. I did something about it. I sat in expectancy, listened for the still, small voice, and waited for a realization of the presence of God. When the realization came, I had attained the mind that was in Christ Jesus. I had reached the Mount of Transfiguration, the consciousness of the Absolute.

If a hundred cases a day come to you, you will have a hundred different forms of treatment or meditation. None of them will be alike. I doubt that you will ever reach the place where you will begin every treatment with the word *is*, even though *is*, is your state of consciousness. But you will have a beautiful experience the moment you say, "Is," and are unable to say another word beyond that or think another thought about what it is or what its nature is. *Is*, is the Middle path: not good humanhood, not bad humanhood, but Christhood.

ACROSS THE DESK

Shortages! Shortages! That is the cry on every hand. What does that mean to us who are students of The Infinite Way? Are we to accept such limitation or is this a call upon us to seek for the spiritual principle involved and put it into practice?

Is God any less God or any less available today than a year ago? Is the flow of God's goodness subject to, and determined by, world conditions? Or is God changeless, eternal, and ever available? Is not this whole earth, which belongs to God, given to us because of divine sonship?

Can wastefulness, stupidity, ineptness, greed, lust for power, in short, the various facets of the carnal mind, obscure God's omnipresent good? Only for those who are ignorant of the principle that all good is embodied in individual consciousness and is, therefore, omnipresent and ever available.

Let us recognize the present world crisis as but another facet of the belief that we can be separated from what we are: infinite God Itself, appearing individually. Let us stand fast in the truth that the carnal mind is not power and can never change the eternal abundance of God's spiritual universe.

Tape Recorded Excerpts
Prepared by the Editor

Many businesses are on rocky ground because the owner considers the business is his business instead of recognizing that "the earth is the Lord's, and the fullness thereof; the world, and they that dwell therein." When he recognizes that, he would see that even the business is a divine activity, governed by infinite wisdom and intelligence and love. The following excerpt will be helpful in achieving a correct perspective.

Business as an Activity of God

"All true and right activity is of God. God is the creative principle of the idea. Whether the idea is an invention, ... a story for a book, ... or one of world peace, if it is an idea of God, God is the creative principle of it. Then we look only to God to maintain it, sustain it, promote it, finance it, give it its reward, gain it its recognition, and ultimately even be the consuming public to utilize it and buy it. ... Since God is the mind of individual being, God, the inventor or creator, appears as God, the ones necessary to the unfoldment."

Joel S. Goldsmith, "The Is No Law of Matter or Disease,"
The 1953 Los Angeles Practitioners' Class.

❖ 7 ❖

Is

GOD IS. THAT is the ultimate of spiritual wisdom. There is only God. Nothing else is; nothing else exists; nothing else has presence; nothing else has power. We could even eliminate the word God and just say, "Is." That which Is, is; and that which Is, is all that is; and the only time that anything can be Is, is now. Is cannot take place yesterday. Is cannot take place tomorrow. The only place for Is, is here; and the only time for Is, is now. Nothing *is* except here, and nothing *is* except now. In that realization we are released instantly from any mental attempt to make anything happen or appear.

Heretofore while we have known, or at least agreed, that God is, we have also undertaken to heal, reform, enrich, or employ those who turn to us for help through some kind of mental or spiritual process. We are released from that in the realization of Is. No one can make something happen in the future, if now is the only time; and if now is God's time, no one can even make something happen now. The whole practice becomes the continuous recognition of Is. Infinity is; immortality is; life is; harmony is; wholeness is; completeness is: "That which I am seeking, I am."[1]

After years of study we come to a state of consciousness where the weight falls off our shoulders and we no longer labor under the heavy responsibility of trying to save anyone. Now we rest in the truth that God's work is done: completeness is; perfection is; harmony is.

113

And what about the world of error? It is the illusion of sense that goes on and will go on forever in the minds of those who struggle under a sense of separation from God and a sense that there is a selfhood apart from God to be redeemed or to be saved.

When we arrive at that state of consciousness, we are the light unto all who turn to us. We cannot be a light running around the universe looking for someone to light up any more than a lighthouse has to run around the ocean looking for ships. It stands still, and the ships seeking guidance look for the lighthouse, just as we stand still and let the world of those ready come to our door.

Grace Appearing as an Acute Need

Readiness for spiritual unfoldment is a matter of Grace, not a matter of free will. There is no one who has the power in and of himself to determine to study eight hours a day. Those who can do that do not have that power of themselves: it has come to them through Grace, so there is no use finding fault with persons who say, "Somehow I don't have time to study truth." They are right; they do not have time because their time is already filled with other things, and the hunger and the thirst for truth have not yet appeared. There is no use trying to fill their hours with truth any more than there is trying to fill a person with food who has already eaten. He will not appreciate it, and it will not taste good, no matter how many hours may have been given to the preparation of it.

So with truth. No one is going to appreciate truth except in proportion to his hunger and thirst for it, and that comes through divine Grace, often manifesting as an acute need. One person finds a need for God or for something to fill a void; another has a need to be healed of a disease; another has a need to be healed of unhappiness or lack. Whatever the acute need is, is divine Grace, because it is compelling him to return home to the Father. Coming down to eating that final meal with the swine drove the Prodigal Son home. This was an evidence of Grace, just as our sins, our diseases, and our lacks are evidences of Grace because those are the problems that may have driven you and me to the work.

Breaking Through the Intellectual Sense to Consciousness

It would be a real achievement if by some supreme sacrifice we could make all our friends, relatives, and neighbors jump into heaven. So far there is no sacrifice that we can make that will bring even one's own husband, wife, or child into heaven until the moment of his hunger and thirst for truth. Therefore, we may as well cease trying to save anyone the interval required for the development of consciousness through which we have gone because we cannot succeed.

It is the part of wisdom not to shock the young student with such absolute statements of truth that he cannot absorb them, and certainly not to expect that even though these truths have been told to him and are repeated tomorrow and the next day that he is going to understand them. Reminders of truth break through the intellectual sense until finally they penetrate consciousness and the student exclaims, "Oh, I see." He then tells us something we have been telling him for years but as if it were something entirely original that he has just discovered that we do not know. He feels that he is sharing a great gift with us, but really it is something that over the years he has not grasped and which now comes to him as his own unfoldment.

Ministering to Individuals on the Level of Their Consciousness

Not only in this letter, but in many of the letters this year, the word *Is* has been emphasized: All already is; harmony already is; and we can rest in that.

It should be apparent, however, that we must come down from cloud nine at least to cloud seven and acknowledge that there are appearances contrary to the state of *Is*, acknowledge that we are dealing with a sick and sinning human race, entertaining a sense of selfhood apart from God. As this hits up against our consciousness, it is also apparent that something must be done about it through our individual work. It will not help those who come to us, nor will it enable us to rise to a healing consciousness, just to sit on cloud nine and repeat, "God is." At this stage we should not try to go beyond the Master Christ Jesus' ministry.

Jesus had a message and a mission for the sick, the dead, the sinning, and to those in ignorance of spiritual light. In ministering to them he was not being very absolute, was he? He was acknowledging a selfhood and a condition apart from God that had to be redeemed through spiritual vision. Jesus was willing to admit that there is the sense of a selfhood apart from the Christ of individual being, and it is that selfhood which has been busy using fishing nets to make its living, whereas in its oneness with the Father it is joint-heir with Christ in God and has never needed to struggle.

Jesus was willing to concede that that sense of separateness brought a sense of separation from good, and the recognition of true identity was his mission.

Transition from
Humanhood to Christhood

What separates the Christ ministry from humanhood is the realization that the world of appearances is not of *My* kingdom, not spiritual reality. None of these appearances ever takes place in heaven. If a volcano or the atomic bomb came and wiped us all out, that would not change one single thing in heaven. God's kingdom would still be intact on earth as it is in heaven. Why? Because this that we behold as humanhood represents a mental concept in human thought, not so much individual human thought but universal belief which we individually accept by virtue of having been born. Human concepts arise from the fact that we were physically conceived and born, and that was our entrance into the whole world of *mis*conception. Now we have to die to that humanhood or misconception.

We have to die so that we can be reborn, but it will not do us any more good to die physically than it has done us any good to be born physically. The death must take place within our consciousness so that we may be reborn of the Spirit. It is a birth that takes place as a transformation in consciousness. A term I like to use is *transition*, the transition from one state of being to another, from one state of consciousness to another.

Transition is what takes place when we begin to perceive that supply is entirely invisible and that what appears out here, whether it is dollar bills or flowers, is but the visible effect of supply. All the outer effects in modern cities, such as skyscrapers, super markets, and banks are not supply. They could easily be wiped out, and nothing would be lost because the supply of that which formed those buildings is in consciousness. "Destroy this temple, and in three days I will raise it up."[2] The same consciousness that placed those buildings there will rebuild them.

That same truth must be realized about personal fortunes and body. If through some unbelief, disbelief, or ignorance, our body, fortune, or our home has been destroyed, let us not be concerned. If we had a crop of fruit and had eaten it, given it away, or the wind had blown it away, we would be ready and waiting for a new crop. The tree is still there, and if the wind blew the tree away, there is life in the earth to develop more trees. Always Consciousness, which is the original essence or substance, is present.

Consciousness Is the Source

Regardless of what effect disappears, it is important to recognize immediately that it is only effect. Cause is invisible. Even the seed is not the cause. That which produced the seed is cause, and a seed is not even necessary. In the first chapter of Genesis, the crops were in the ground before there were any seeds. Consciousness is the source. Consciousness could just as well appear as a full-grown plant and produce a seed for the next generation as it could produce a seed and then produce a flower.

All form, all figure, and all effect emanate from consciousness. When we say, "Is," we are not talking about an effect: we are talking about Consciousness, the Source of all that is. We are not looking at a sick person and saying he is well; we are not looking at depletion and saying it is completion. When we say, "Is," we are talking about God, Consciousness, Source, Cause and noting that It *is*.

The degree of Consciousness realized determines whether it is going to take forty days for the crop to appear or whether the crop may instantaneously appear in the realization of Is. It need not take forty days, but if it does, let us not be concerned about it. That merely represents the degree of our ability to perceive the Is already manifest. We are fortunate to be of those who know that Is, *is*, that Consciousness *is*, even though it is necessary to let this truth operate in individual consciousness until the fruitage of it begins to appear.

If our patient or student does not have an instantaneous healing or if he does not grasp the truth in the first year or in the tenth year, let that not concern us. We must be loving and patient, forgiving his dropping away seventy times seventy because until a person grasps the truth, we cannot expect him to be unswervingly true to it. There will be a falling away; and there will be a dropping away. That has nothing to do with you or with me: it has to do with accepting all those who come to us even if they are returning after the seventieth time. There may be degrees of falling or dropping away which may be difficult to forgive, and we cannot immediately accept Judas back into our innermost circle, but we can accept him back on the outer plane and continue giving of our best.

Why Some Students
Receive More Attention

There are always serious students who want a great deal of a teacher's time, effort, and thought, and it is those to whom he wishes to give the utmost of himself. Sometimes he is puzzled because there are others also demanding a great deal of his time, and he wonders how all this can be done. I give much time and effort to those I feel are not only hungering and thirsting after truth but who indicate their sincerity by their actions. They do not merely take up all my time and let me pour out on them, but when they are not with me they are studying diligently and seriously, and listening hard. They are putting themselves into the work: they are not merely coming as a blotter to absorb what I have to give and then going away and expecting to come back the next time as a fresh blotter. When I observe students who make their dedication very evident, and from their questions and talk I can tell that they are really putting in time, effort, study, and devotion, those are the ones to whom I give the most of myself. The others receive less and less all the way down to those who never have an opportunity for an appointment.

Very often students have said, "I don't know how you ever get to see Joel. He just won't see anybody." And then you can know that, as far as Joel is concerned, they have made it evident that all they want is the healing of the moment, and they are putting nothing of themselves into this activity. I do not refuse to give them spiritual help. They can telephone me and they can come to public lectures and closed classes, but they will have a very difficult time obtaining a personal appointment. The reason? They are giving no evidence that they are putting themselves into the work or that God is their aim rather than what can be obtained through God. My judgment on this score is not infallible. I have taken in and been taken in. I have had many to whom I have given time, attention, thought, and effort, who have not fulfilled themselves, but I would rather make a mistake in that direction than bar anyone who might possibly be sincere in his endeavors.

As the student continues on this path, it becomes very clear after awhile that there is nothing to be gained but God Itself. If an abundance of health and a great amount of wealth were added, the student would not know what to do with them. He would have no awareness of health; he would just be aware of a body that seemed to function. Wealth would be unimportant because no person can eat more than three meals a day or needs more than a simple place to live. Very soon he learns that there is nothing to be accomplished through the work except the joy of experiencing God and the companionship of those who are finding themselves home in God.

We who glimpse one tiny bit of Is become the light unto a certain part of the world, and we have no right to judge or bar those seeking that light, but we must divide our so-called human time so that we give the utmost of it to those with a deep hunger and thirst after truth, rather than merely after effects. Let us be wise in that, very wise.

From the first day I entered the practice, I made a rule that no one could be on my telephone more than three minutes unless it were a very unusual circumstance. The telephone must be kept open so that students or patients do not have to call six, eight, ten, or twelve times and find the line busy. The reason a person reaches out is to touch consciousness. There is no need for him to rehearse his family or bodily history. It may be a comfort to him on the first visit or the first call to unburden himself, but after that there is no excuse except in a most unusual circumstance for anything that one, two, three, or four minutes cannot take care of. Any rehearsal of the error that was repeated yesterday is not only a waste of time, but sometimes prevents healing.

There is only one thing for a person to do once he has unburdened himself of his problems, and that is to seek truth, not a rehearsal of the error. So after the first call, the student should either ask for more help or more truth, and in two or three minutes a practitioner can give truth sufficient for the need of that moment. There are always exceptions that come up in individual problems, but wisdom shows those.

It is not a rehearsal of the error that brings healing. It is the devotion of consciousness to truth and the opportunity for it to be active. The individual who is merely calling to repeat the error is not only depriving himself, he is depriving the practitioner and the rest of the patients or students. Our recognition is, Is, so what difference does all this other business make?

Appearances as Temptation

We have Is. But we also have appearances. All forms of error are appearances, suggestion, or temptation. Is any one of those three a thing or a person? Then where can a suggestion be? In human thought. Where can a temptation be? In human thought. Where can an appearance be? In human thought. Does any one of those three have substance or law? No.

We are absolute in our realization that Is, *is*. Is, is now; Is, is always; and Is, is Spirit, Life, Truth, Love. But we do recognize that out here are the sinner, the poor in spirit, the ignorant, the unillumined, and the dead. They do not exist as reality. How could God have created an old person, a withered person, a poor person? There is no such thing. But as far as we are concerned they exist as long as we see, hear, taste, touch, or smell them. As long as they keep coming to our consciousness they exist for us, but they do not exist as entities or identity, as person or thing. They exist as suggestion or temptation.

It is reported that the Master had three temptations, but let us not think that those were his only temptations. "And when the devil had ended all the temptation, he departed from him for a season."[3] It does not state that Satan left him. No, Satan left him *for a season*. Always he came back to the Master. Satan was with Jesus in the garden of Gethsemane, tempting him to believe in approaching tests and death. In God's kingdom no such thing could have happened. "Let this cup pass from me."[4] Let what cup pass? The temptation that he might go through even a temporary experience of death or disgrace.

Not Denials but Is

As long as we are faced with this world, we will be faced with Satan tempting us to believe in those in prison, those in sin, or those in sickness, and until we come to the point of rebirth we will accept these appearances as something to do something about, instead of knowing the truth that makes free. The truth is, Is—all else, mental concepts. A mental concept has no substantial form. It has an illusory form. A mental concept or a suggestion has only the appearance or substance of temptation for us to accept, believe in, or try to do something about.

When someone tells us he is ill, and our response is that that is illusion, we have given the treatment because we cannot do anything to an illusion. If we were to see the leaves on a flowerpot as green snakes and then realized that they are not snakes but illusion, would we sit down and give

ourselves a treatment? The treatment is the recognition that
what we thought was evil has only an illusory existence. The
moment we recognize that the problem exists only as temptation, our treatment is over.

Let us come to the realization that since Is, is, all else
is not, even if we have to sit down for an hour and remind
ourselves of all the statements of truth we know. We are not
removing or changing something out here; we are not saving
a person's life, we are not reducing a fever. We are coming to
a point of conviction within ourselves that Is, is.

When we behold any form of error through the senses
of sight, hearing, taste, touch, or smell, we will no longer
deny it. Looking at a pot full of what appear to be dangerous
green snakes is the picture being presented to us. We know
their destructive and deadly nature and we know people who
have been bitten by them and died quickly in pain. It makes
no difference whether it is a snake or whether it is somebody
with cancer, tuberculosis, or poverty, even though we know
about the universal belief in the incurability of cancer, the
horribleness of tuberculosis, the despair of poverty, and the
ferocity of sin. In our metaphysical state of consciousness we
are tempted to say that it is not true because God never made
it. Yet it still keeps bobbing up. There is no benefit, nor is
there any healing power in denying it.

Looking at a beautiful plant and just saying that there are
no snakes there does not do anything to the plant. Neither
does it do anything to us because denying it does not fill us
with the realization of what is there. In our hypnotized state,
we do not know that a plant is there but we are denying
that there are snakes there, and we have nothing. The great
miracle in healing work and in living is that when we are
confronted with the vicious "snake" of cancer or tuberculosis

we can look at it and say, "Is. It is." We are not denying it. We know we would not be seeing snakes if there were nothing there. There is something there and our denying whatever is there is not going to change it one single bit. So we are going to look right into that den of snakes, "Yes, there is something there that is an activity of God-consciousness. I cannot deny it; I must acknowledge it! God is; it is.

I do not know the nature of its being; but I know that it is being because I see it there. I feel it there. I smell it. I know it is there. It exists. Now, Father, what am I beholding? What is really there?"

With that we have set up a vacuum within us; we have not set up a vacuum out there. We do not have a world of nothingness now to be eliminated. We do not have a world out here that is an illusion that we want to get rid of. Now we have Is out here, Is made manifest, God-consciousness made manifest. Even though we do not yet know its name or nature, it is. "Now, Father, what?"

Inside of us, we have made room for the Father to reveal to us what is, and all of a sudden our eyes clear and we see a beautiful plant. Where there was a cancer, where there was tuberculosis, where there was paralysis, instead of wiping it all out and merely saying that it is an illusion, which does nothing to anybody, now we know that since God is, God fills all space, so there is something there, and it is of God. We do not know its name or nature, but whereas before we saw "through a glass, darkly,"[5] now by acknowledging that we are seeing something and turning to the Father for what is, suddenly we see "face to face."[5] The false appearances goes and we behold it as it is.

If God is, harmony is, perfection is. No amount of treatment will make it so, but spiritual realization reveals it. That is the dying to appearances and the rebirth to seeing "through a glass, darkly" and then ultimately "face to face." Spiritual regeneration comes when we stop denying this world and calling it an illusion. The only illusion about the world is our concept of the world. The world is God expressed. This is God's universe, and that is what Jesus came to reveal. Yet here is a world of people with discords, inharmonies, crime, slavery, and sin. Why? Because of ignorance of the truth, because of judging by finite appearance.

Individually we are unlimited. We cannot be bound to any place, any circumstance, or any condition. There are no limits because we are consciousness. We are not body: we are consciousness. We have omnipresence instantaneously, here, there, and the other place, the moment we rise above the limitation of a little piece of body in which we are supposed to be living. Some day we will see that the body lives in consciousness.

There is no more limit to our being than there is to our imagination. Our imagination is closer to the real than what we call common sense because in our imagination we wander back into the millions of years past and we can wander into the millions of years of the future. The vision of the men who saw the coming of the submarine and the airplane was the vision of people who could not be limited to just seeing what was going on around them in time and space. They had a faculty beyond that.

Let us have the vision to look at any thing or person that exists out here and come to the conclusion that all that is, is God expressing and manifesting Itself. Let us not give it a label, but see it for what it is: Is, Life. It is an activity of Life going on, an activity of Consciousness, expressing as form. What it is we do not know. If we ask for illumination on it, soon as we look up we will be able to say, "Before I saw 'through a glass, darkly,' and it looked like a cancer. Now I see 'face to face,' and where the cancer appeared to be, there is the offspring of God." No amount of standing on that Is will make it so, but it will bring us to seeing that it is so.

"The Lord Is My Shepherd"

"Is" and "Judge not" are very much alike as principles, because in both "Is" and "Judge not," we look at any appearance or claim, whatever its name or nature, and ignore it, look through it to the fact that only God is the reality. If there were nothing more in the 23ʳᵈ Psalm, than "The Lord is my shepherd,"[6] that would be enough, because that tells us, "You do not have to reach out to God. You do not have to make contact with God. You do not have to win God's mercy or gain God's ear. Already the Lord is your shepherd. That which you would attempt through prayer or by other means to achieve, already is. 'The Lord is my shepherd. I shall not want ' "

"I shall not want." Why? "The Lord is my shepherd." There is no use now trying to overcome lack or to treat for supply. The only treatment is: "Thank You, Father. You are my shepherd. How can I want? You are leading me, not will lead me or that I deserve to be led, but You lead me beside the still waters and make me lie down in green pastures." Not only do we not have to coerce God, but He is chasing us harder than we are chasing Him. If only we could stop praying long enough to let God catch up with us, we would find that our need would be met long before we even knew that we had any need. But we are so busy chasing God that we are far ahead of Him.

The one way to slow down is with the word, Is. "The Lord is my shepherd." Let us sit patiently and let that Is catch up; let that Is come into expression or manifestation. Not only does the Lord lead us beside the still waters, He *makes* us lie down in green pastures. Heretofore, we have believed that it was necessary to win God's mercy, gain God's goodness, bribe God or tithe for God, and promise to be good. And all the time the 23rd Psalm assures us that the Lord *is* our shepherd. Not only is that the truth but we do not have to persuade or ask Him to bring us to green pastures. He *makes* us lie down in them, even when we are obstinate and try to stay out of His reach.

This Psalm brings a deeper realization of the great truth that harmony already is. It is a matter of opening our consciousness and becoming receptive and responsive to everything that is already a part of our infinite divine Consciousness.

As we learn the *is-ness* of God and open up our inner consciousness to let the wisdom flow from within, It will operate in our outer world to bring harmony in body, business, being, and in every other area. It does not mean that we will change everybody who comes into our world. Many of them we will have to let go and watch them go because if they cannot adapt themselves to the Spirit, sooner or later we will be led away from them. We just cannot change everybody in the world; we cannot reform everybody; we cannot make spiritual people out of everybody because this may not be their time. But this is our time, and we have been led to this moment.

I have nothing that will benefit anybody except those who come of their own accord. If I have to draw them in, I have nothing for them, and they cannot understand my language.

But if they come, the Father drew them, and the Father drew them to receive something, and they will receive it.

We can sit still without ever making a human move and be led every step of the way. John Burroughs has said it so wisely: "My own shall come to me... as the rivers flow to the sea." We wait; we do not hurry or make haste. Why? Because there is a God, and God has ordained good to Its creation. Let us accept the truth: God already is; good already is; love already is; harmony already is; peace already is; and then be still and let it flow.

Let us learn to be still, learn to meditate, and learn to accept the truth that God is love, that He is our shepherd and leads us every moment of the way.

Across the Desk

Very seldom did Joel speak of contentment, but underneath all the great activity of his days and nights, there was a pervading spirit of contentment, a feeling of joy in each moment at being an instrument for the Divine, a satisfaction in doing to the full whatever was given him to do.

Each of us on the spiritual path may be at a different state and stage of consciousness, and indeed each of us may find himself in varying states and stages of consciousness in any given period of time. It is not given to any of us to maintain a continuous mountaintop consciousness, and for each of us there are valley experiences, too. There may be moment of being at a very high point of clarity and inspiration and other moments of discouraging barrenness. If, however, we can stand back occasionally, withdraw for a few moments from the scene, and turn within to the deep pool of contentment within, which is always there awaiting our discovery, we will be renewed and restored and be given the courage to go forward on our journey.

TAPE RECORDED EXCERPTS
Prepared by the Editor

Is not every problem really a problem of supply: supply of health, money, morals, joy? The following excerpts will help you gain a greater awareness of the real nature of supply and its omnipresence so that you will never be mesmerized by the temptation to accept limitation in any of its forms.

Omnipresent Supply

"No one can ever lessen supply because God Itself is the supply. There is no such thing as God giving supply or God sending supply. If you had a billion dollars and did not have God, you would have nothing. We have had people with a million dollars who could not even eat a meal. When you have the forms of supply without the supply itself, you have nothing. ...

"As we begin to perceive that God is our individual consciousness and that God is infinite, we perceive the nature of supply as that which is invisible, and we no longer judge by appearances as to the amount of our supply. ... When experiences come, ... such as in the midst of war or sudden depressions, where there is a temporary absence of forms of supply, then with this wisdom the years of the locust are quickly restored and the flow begins... to come. ...

"There is an invisible activity going on within me, which is an activity of Truth in my consciousness. That activity of Truth in my consciousness is renewing me, day by day—physically, mentally, morally, financially. Whatever is necessary for my earthly experience, this inner consciousness is renewing day by day. Day by day the manna falls; day by day this inner Selfhood which is my invisible being is manufacturing the particular form of coconuts that I may need for daily experience."

Joel S. Goldsmith, "The Invisible Nature of Your Life,"
The 1955 First Kailua Study Group.

"There is no way to demonstrate supply... and the reason is that all the supply that exists in heaven or in earth exists now within you. Any attempt to demonstrate it must result in failure. There is not any outside of you, and if you want to enjoy the abundance of supply, you must open out a way for that supply to escape. How you do it is going to be a matter between you and your communion with God. It may be that you have been holding on too tightly to money, and you are going to have to learn how to let loose of it, and by turning it loose, set in motion the flow that is to come to you. The bread that you cast upon the water is the bread that comes back to you. It is not your neighbor's bread: it is your own bread. ... If you do not cast it upon the water, you have none coming back to you, because all the bread on the water is ear-marked to come back to the person who sent it forth."

Joel S. Goldsmith, "Basis of Healing Work,"
The 1956 Second Chicago Closed Class.

* 8 *

MIND IMBUED WITH TRUTH

ALL SPIRITUAL HEALING depends on the degree of evolved or developed spiritual consciousness that a person has attained. To the medical way of thinking, a man or woman is a physical body, and a physician may go further and acknowledge that the mind has something to do with the body. The general conclusion is that if a person has the right mental attitude along with some medicine, he is going to be made well, which is correct from a *materia medica* point of view. On the material and mental level of life there must be specific remedies for the discords of sense.

When you present yourself to a practitioner, however, he does not examine your mind or your body. Why? He has arrived at a state of evolved and developed consciousness that enables him to see you as you really are: spiritual. And not only are you spiritual but the entire universe, including your body, is spiritual. Because of the practitioner's evolved spiritual consciousness and your making yourself one with it, you respond to that higher consciousness and are lifted above the five physical senses. The Son of God, the Christ, is raised up in you. Material sense drops away, and with it the false images of physical sense which we call disease, unhappiness, or lack.

Evolved Spiritual
Consciousness Discerns True Being

To the evolved and developed spiritual consciousness, you are not seen as a human being made up partly of good and partly of evil, partly of mind and partly of matter. This is because the evolved spiritual consciousness is not looking at your body; it is not looking at your mind: it is communing with you; it knows you as the child of God. Wherever there is an evolved spiritual awareness, there is a discernment of your true being, your true nature, and it is for this reason that healing at the spiritual level is without effort. No suggestions are thrown at you for the purpose of convincing you or changing your state of mind.

Spiritual consciousness does not take you into consideration, for there is no you separate and apart from God and God's spiritual kingdom. The evolved or developed spiritual consciousness is not thinking of treating or healing you. It is you who are reaching this consciousness and seeking for help, but this consciousness is realizing only God, one infinite Being, infinitely manifested. It has evolved to the place where it ignores appearances.

A person might get into serious difficulty, however, by having appearances ignored by someone who was using the words without having the consciousness to back them up. The words themselves will not heal anybody; the words themselves will not do anything. It is the consciousness that does it, and that consciousness must have the spiritual discernment to see that there are not two powers. God, being infinite Spirit, is omnipotent; therefore, there are not two powers. No one has to battle anything or overcome anything. He has nothing to rise above. In spiritual consciousness there is only the realization:

God is. There is no other power; there is no other presence; there is no other being; there is no other law. In that realization, the law of infection, contagion, or accident does not operate.

Nobody knows how spiritual healing takes place. Nobody of spiritual consciousness knows how he is going to work on a particular case, what the results are going to be, or when. It is a constant living in the awareness of God as individual being. A developed spiritual consciousness lives in that awareness always, not merely when a person asks for help. It has to be a twenty-four hour a day realization. The statement that God is the only power cannot be turned on and off. A person on the path must live in that consciousness continuously, so that no matter how many times a day other powers are presented to him, they do not register. When he lives always in the consciousness of God as the only power, then what the world calls healing takes place.

Human Good and
Human Evil Are Both Illusory

Human experience, sometimes called the Adamic dream, is a state of mortal illusion with sin, disease, death, lack, and limitation its products. Most persons do not realize that the harmonious and good part of that dream is just as illusory as the inharmonious. In The Infinite Way, therefore, I not only emphasize that sin, disease, and death are states of mesmeric illusion, but that physical health and material wealth are equally mesmeric illusion. Students must rise above physical harmony as much as they rise above physical discords until they reach the altitude or atmosphere of spiritual harmony. When do they reach that atmosphere? Never, as long as they believe their life is dependent on their heart, liver, lungs, or brain.

A heart that beats at a normal rate is just as much an illusory sense as a heart that is abnormal. The diseased or abnormal heart can become normal, and the normal heart can become abnormal. The condition of a heart or for that matter the condition of any organ of the body can change, so it all must be a part of the fabric of the dream, the fabric of nothingness, the fabric of hypnotism. The mere fact that a human being can be completely well one minute and drop dead the next must be evidence that the entire fabric of human experience is illusory.

Good health is just as much an illusion as is poor health. Wealth is just as much an illusion as is poverty if wealth is dependent upon the number of dollars a person possesses. Dollars can disappear. You not only can lose them in investments or in property, but the government can change radically or go out of existence, as governments have done before, and your money is then wiped out.

If you think of your money as wealth, you may wake up someday and be disillusioned. If you think by having a doctor tell you you are in perfect health that you have demonstrated spiritual wholeness, you may be in for disillusionment. Health does change to sickness; wealth does change to poverty; and virtue does change to vice. Anyone whose faith is in his heart, liver, lungs, or body, anyone whose faith is in the amount of his bank account, or anyone who relies solely on the fact that a person is good, is living in a state of delusion.

Illusion Is Never Externalized

Does this mean that your body or your wealth is illusion? No, it means that your *sense* of it is the illusion. Your belief that harmony is in the body or in the bank account is the illusion. Your money is not an illusion and your body is not an illusion. It is your sense of them that is the illusion, and that sense is never externalized. It is always in the mind.

When you look at the railroad tracks that seem to come together in the distance and somebody says, "Don't believe it. That's an illusion," you do not think that the illusion is in the railroad tracks. No, you assume that the rails are in perfect order all the way to the end of the line. The illusory sense of their coming together is in your mind.

When you stand at the water's edge and see the sky coming down to the water, you know that it is an illusion. Yet you do not believe that the scene in front of you is an illusion. The illusion is in your perception of what you are beholding. Does that add up?

Where is an illusion at all times? Within you, within your own mind. When someone says to you, "I am sick," and you know that that is an illusion, does that mean that the person is an illusion or his body is an illusion? No, it means that if you believe what he tells you or shows you, you are suffering from an illusion. If you believe what you see, hear, taste, touch, or smell about anyone, that is illusion.

But it could be just as much an illusion if a person were to say to you, "I am well." If you were a skeptic, you might wonder whether or not he has a doctor's verdict to prove it. He looks well and may not have a pain, but what would his doctor say? Even if the doctor said he was well, that verdict would only be based on an illusory concept or material sense of body which *materia medica* entertains.

The Recognition of the Illusory Nature of an Appearance Destroys It

There have been many times when persons have been so ill with a fever that they were sure they could not fulfill some pressing obligation, but they asked for spiritual help, and the fever abated. What happened to the fever? When the picture of a man with a fever was presented to me, I did not give him any medicine or do anything of a material or physical nature. But the fever left. Where did it go? Where was it? It was an illusion in human belief, and when I refused to accept it as reality, it dropped dead. Had I accepted the fever as truth it would have continued.

Error continues forever unless it hits up against a state of consciousness that does not accept it. Then one with God is a majority. The world was supposed to be flat, a square world. For thousands of years it stayed that way until Columbus came along and the flatness or squareness began to dissolve and disappear. Where was it square? In the illusory sense of it. Did Christopher Columbus change it? Not one single bit. Today it is the way it was when the people of his day saw it and believed it to be flat. Now our concept is nearer to the truth.

At one time it was believed that the sun revolved around the earth. That was illusion, but was the illusion ever externalized? No, the illusion existed in universal belief or universal human thought. But let us suppose that in my ignorance I believe the sun goes around the earth, thereby making that belief mine. Or suppose I believe I am ill and I make that a part of me by accepting that belief. I have then taken it out of the universal and made it personal to me, and I will be ill unless I can find someone who will agree to disagree, who will refuse to accept the disease even though I can show it to him, someone who will stand back and say, "Now wait a minute. How can this be? If there is a God and God is infinite, then this cannot be." You have to have the same vision that Christopher Columbus had in looking at a flat world, a vision that does not merely see through the mind but that has an intuitive sense which sees through the appearance.

Suppose I look out at an audience and see people, old people. That is what the eyes tell me. But what does my developed spiritual awareness tell me? There is nothing out there but the life of God. What happens when I perceive that? The sick begin to feel well again. The old begin to be young again. There are many examples of people who have reached seventy-five, eighty, eighty-five, ninety, or ninety-five years of age, who are not decrepit, not deaf, dumb, or blind. Some have caught the nature of their true identity, and their body is no longer under the law of matter, but under Grace. When the body is under Grace, Grace maintains it as long as a person has need for it. The material sense of body has arisen because of the Adamic belief in two powers. This material sense of body is lost in proportion as God is realized as infinite Spirit, the Substance, Law, and Activity of the whole universe, including the body.

One person on a platform can bring forth healing for a hundred persons in an audience if they are receptive and do not come in an argumentative or defiant mood, but as a little child with the attitude, "Let your spiritual vision touch me."

There are lecturers and teachers who are such spiritually developed men and women that when they are on a platform somebody receives a healing. It may be only one or two although it could be ten, twelve, or a hundred if they were all receptive. The lecturer or teacher knows that all sense of humanhood is illusory whether it is good or bad so he does not try to change it. He realizes the invisible Christ-health or the invisible Christ-sense of supply, the invisible spiritual being which I am and you are, which is not young, middle-aged, or old, but eternally the Son of God. When an individual refuses to accept the appearance of good health or abundant supply or refuses to accept bad health or a lack of supply as permanent, but is willing to hold to the truth that what he sees with his eyes and what he hears with his ears is an illusory sense, healing takes place.

Is Your Mind Imbued with Truth?

What you know in your heart is truth. And what do you know in your heart? God made all that was made, and all that God made was good. God constitutes individual being, your being and mine. Even your body is the temple of the living God. I cannot see that with my eyes but inwardly I have discerned that that is the truth. Everyone who practices spiritual healing has discerned that truth or he could never be successful. Successful practitioners have discerned the truth that they must not believe what they see even when it looks good. Inwardly they hold to the spiritual reality which is God and God's creation.

If my mind is imbued with truth and has received the truth that I and the Father are one and that spiritual reality is the only reality, then that mind imbued with truth becomes the law unto the health of those who come to me. The mind of the practitioner imbued with truth makes a treatment effective. The unillumined mind, the mind of a person not imbued with truth, the mind that has never studied and practiced spiritual truth, cannot heal anything. That mind cannot bless except humanly. That mind cannot bring about health, supply, or harmony in individual experience. A good human being might do favors humanly: he might give a person money, he might pay for his vacation, but spiritu- ally he has no power to benefit the person. That same good human being, however, after a year spent with his mind and heart and soul in spiritual literature and scripture, with his mind now imbued with truth, becomes a law of health and healing unto those who reach out to him.

The degree of your reading or hearing the word determines the measure of the consciousness that ultimately evolves. If you were born with an evolved spiritual consciousness, you would not have to read books and you would not have to listen to tapes or attend classes. If this consciousness had evolved from within naturally, you would be a healer without having had to develop the consciousness. But there is not one person like that in a million. Each person evolves from the human state into which he was born, through his study, reading, and practicing, until he attains some measure of the higher consciousness.

If you are new to truth, do not be surprised if you cannot heal. If after several years of study, however, you cannot do healing work, begin to examine yourself to see if you have just read books and felt a little flurry of something or whether you have really studied to know the principles and practiced them until your consciousness was lifted to where it no longer believed that the sky sits on the ocean or that railroad tracks come together, and was able instinctively to look through that appearance to what actually is there.

Seeing Through Mesmeric Pictures

A very important point to remember is that a practitioner does not heal you; a practitioner does not reform or enrich you: you are already those things. Christopher Columbus did not make the world round. He proved it to be round.

In reality, you are the offspring of God, heir of God, and "joint-heir with Christ"[1] to all the heavenly riches. You are in the kingdom of God now. Your body is the temple of the living God now; your business is the temple of the living God; your family is the temple of the living God. Your home is the temple because God constitutes all that God made. God is the reality of your being, your body, your business, your home, your family, your health, your supply, your profession, your talent. God constitutes these, therefore you can realize:

My body is the temple of the living God. My business is the temple of the living God. My art, my profession, my home, my family life, my community life—these are the temple. God raised them up, and God maintains and sustains them.

After years of study, you may look out and see a wrecked temple—physical, mental, moral, or financial. But you do not believe in appearances because you know that appearances are only the product of the mesmeric illusion, like the sky sitting on the water, the tracks coming together in the distance, or the mirage out in the desert. You know that those mesmeric pictures exist only in universal belief. Instead of fearing and hating them, now you look right through them and say, "I know thee who thou art: the fabric of nothingness, the fabric of hypnotism, the son of your father, the devil—nothingness, no power, no presence."

Thus by not believing in or accepting appearances, but consciously rejecting them and refusing to entertain them and with even a trace of spiritual discernment, you know that there could not possibly be God and a wrecked temple, especially when God created that temple to begin with, and God is its law, its creator, maintainer, sustainer, and the substance of it. Your mind imbued with truth is the law unto any situation. But your mind when it is the unillumined human, unimbued with truth, can only look out at that sky sitting on the water and feel the limitation of the horizon. That is all the unillumined human mind can see.

The Appearance Is a State of Hypnotism

The pioneers of metaphysical truth have revealed the importance of not judging by appearances but judging righteous judgment. Do not judge, criticize, or condemn after the seeing of the eye for that is only the picture of the unillumined, mesmeric mind, the mind of ignorance, which neither sees, hears, tastes, touches, nor smells correctly. To judge righteous judgment means to have such an inner developed spiritual sense that if you were called upon to go into a prison to help a prisoner you would not go there judging, condemning, hating, or fearing him, but with a "Father, forgive him, for he knows not what he does. This is Thy beloved child in spite of appearances." Metaphysicians do not visit prisons to reform sinners, to pity the prisoners, or to preach to them, but to reveal to them their true identity.

God has raised up His temple, which this world is, and it is perfect. You do not have to pray to God to heal a person. You have to bear witness to the truth that God constitutes the person. God is the very temple of his body, his health, his wealth, his business, or profession. In spite of the ugly appearance, if you can hold to the truth with your spiritual vision, suddenly you will realize that the appearance was just a state of hypnotism. There is no city out there in the desert. That is a mirage. Some inner thing will convince you that water on the desert is not water, so you go forward, splashing right through the water that is not there. Why? Because you have discerned that the nature of that water on the desert is illusion.

Live by Grace

One day you will discern that the nature of sin, disease, death, and all physicality, even good physicality, is illusion. Man does not live by heart beats. Man does not live by bread alone. Man lives by the grace of God.

Grace, Thy grace, is my sufficiency in all things. By Thy grace I live; by Thy grace I eat; by Thy grace I assimilate and eliminate. By Thy grace I survive. By Thy grace I am eternal, not by bread, not by money, not by a heart, a liver, or lungs. My heart, liver, and lungs live because I have the grace of God.

You have money in your pocket because of the grace of God. Having money is not evil. It is the misplaced faith in it that is the evil. If you put your faith in money, you have made a god of it. So, also, if you put your faith in a heart, liver, or lungs, you have made a god out of it. You will be just as disappointed one day with that heart, liver, or those lungs as you ever can be with money. Do not put your faith in anything external. Put your faith in Grace. By the grace of God, your body is the temple of the living God, not by virtue of vitamins or minerals. You can take vitamins or minerals as a food supplement, but you do not live by them any more than you live by eating meat, vegetables, or by drinking milk. You live by the grace of God. So, too, you may have all the money in the world if there is any need for it, but you do not live by it. The money comes by the grace of God, and you live by that Grace. If money is necessary you will have it.

"Know ye not that ye are the temple of God, and that the Spirit of God dwelleth in you?"[2] Your body is the temple of the living God; so it your business and everything that concerns you.

My student body is the temple of the living God, and I treat it sacredly. My work is the temple of the living God, and it cannot be defiled.

I Appears as
Whatever Form Is Necessary

You live by every word of God that you entertain in consciousness. If that Word appears as food on your table, money in your pocket, good business, or a spiritual ministry, well and good. But if you find yourself in the middle of the ocean with only a rubber boat, do not be concerned. You still are the temple of the living God. God is still there, and even there you will live by the grace of God. It was forty years in the wilderness for Moses. Anywhere you may be, remember that you are not living by effect, but by *I*, by virtue of the truth that *I* in the midst of you is mighty; and that *I* was planted in the midst of you by the grace of God. It will appear as whatever form is necessary to your experience at any given moment.

My mind, which was the mind of a businessman who knew no spiritual truth, imbued with truth, became a law of health and supply unto all those who came to me. The day will come when, as a businessman, a businesswoman, or a housewife, your mind imbued with truth will become a law of resurrection to many a dying person, a law of resurrection to many lost fortunes and lost employments, a law of resurrection to health, harmony, and wholeness. What does this? Your mind imbued with truth. Then some of your friends and relatives come by and say, "Why, I knew you when you were—"

"Yes, I know all about it. You knew me when I was the unillumined human mind. But what you don't know is that

I died. I died. I have been reborn by virtue of the truth that now fills the same mind that was once occupied with pleasures and amusements."

Overcome the World
of Mental Concepts

An illusion is never objectified. Your body is not an illusion; this world is not an illusion. When I say that this world is an illusion, I am referring to Jesus' statement that this world of human concepts is the illusion—not the world out there. The world in the mind is the illusion. Jesus called it "this world": "My kingdom is not of this world."[3] Later he spoke of overcoming that world, but even after he had overcome the world, there were no mountains, lakes, or oceans missing. In fact, nothing was missing from the world, not even any dictators. They are still here just as they were in his day. What then did Jesus mean when he said, "I have overcome the world."[4] He meant that he had overcome the world of illusion in the mind: "My world is now pure. It is the temple of the living God. If you want to despoil the temple and continue with your animal sacrifices, your selling of doves, and your money changing, go ahead, but I have overcome that world. I do not live in it. My peace, I have."

That was not the peace the world can give, not the peace that comes with a heart that beats rhythmically, not the peace that comes from knowing you have an income of so many dollars, not the peace that comes because you have a happy family. Those things make for the peace the world can give, and Jesus did not have any of that peace. His family had deserted him. He did not know where to lay his head.

He had none of the things of "this world," but he had an inner peace. He had overcome the world of illusion within himself. He could look out and see that the sky did not sit on the mountain, and see beyond the graveyard to immortality. That is the difference between the unillumined human mind, the mind that knows nothing of spiritual truth, and the mind that is imbued with truth.

Imbued with truth, the mind is no longer a human mind. It is spiritual consciousness. The human mind has died, died to its illusion, died to the fabric of hypnotism. Now it looks out and does not see that hypnotic picture. "I shall be satisfied, when I awake, with thy likeness."[5] When you awaken you will see the person as he is, and you will be satisfied with that likeness. You will not try to change him or reform him or improve him. You will see him as he is.

Mesmeric Sense Arises
Out of a Belief in Good and Evil

Right now we are in the kingdom of God. What appears as sin, disease, lack, and limitation is only a mesmeric state, the state that came in with our acceptance of two powers: good and evil. That is what makes us look at each other and see young and old, tall and short, thin and stout. It is that mesmeric sense which had its foundation in the acceptance of the belief in good and evil. When you stop being frightened at the appearance of sin, disease, death, lack, or limitation and begin to see through it, it does not frighten you. You know now that it does not exist out there. It exists in human belief, and if you want to nullify it you had better not accept it. Error is destroyed when it meets up with one individual who does not accept evil as a power.

When you find those who have been schooled to the point where they do not believe in the mirage on the desert, you also find beautiful healing work. They have seen through the mirage, and this world does not sadden them any more. They have seen that temporal power is not power and that spiritual power is the only power. Only Spirit is power, and Spirit does not contend against bombs, dictators, governments, or any other form of stupidity.

There is no duality in the grace of God because the mesmeric sense of two powers has been dispelled. Even though I look out at the students in a class and, as far as my eyes are concerned, see them appearing as physical form, I am not fooled by it. The mesmerism has dropped away from me so that I know them as they are: incorporeal, spiritual, pure, eternal, the temple of God. Not only do I see them as they are, spiritual and perfect, but in some measure they, too, see me that way because they are not looking at the frame of a man. They feel the rhythm of God, the spirit of God, which is flowing out. The rhythm of God has nothing to do with physical sensation or with vibrations. The rhythm of God is a ceaseless flowing.

The rhythm of God that I feel in students because of their love of God makes us one in the common bond of a love of God. Every teacher of the Spirit has had built for him a temple of the living God which is his ministry, his student body, or his practice. God builds that temple for each of us whether it is a profession or a business, and we welcome into that temple those who are like-minded. Students select as their teacher the one who has had more of the veil of illusion stripped away from him. The aim and ambition of all students should be to pierce the veil of mesmerism, behold this universe as it is, and then be satisfied with that likeness.

Across the Desk

Problems always present themselves in the form of pictures as the human scene parades itself before us. We see a serious accident; someone reports a disease in need of healing or a sick business to be restored, and all these are pictures etched on the human mind, crying out to be corrected, healed, or adjusted in some way.

Hypnotism operates as pictures: good and bad, happy and sad. We can let the pictures come and go as they appear as our human experience. The secret of keeping ourselves de-hypnotized, however, is to feel no inner reaction to any of them. In proportion to our lack of reaction, are we untouched. To keep ourselves de-hypnotized, we turn within to make contact with our Source.

As we let go of the human picture, with whatever it suggestion may be, the pictures are left outside. They fall away in the presence of the realized Christ-consciousness attained in meditation. In the inner sanctuary, this sacred temple of *I AM*, no picture enters. The deep silence carries with it its peace and benediction.

Tape Recorded Excerpts
Prepared by the Editor

Business as an Activity of God
(continued from the June letter)

"In real estate, if we see God… as the only landlord, then we see God as the only tenant: not two, not a landlord and tenant, but God appearing as landlord and God appearing as tenant, one simultaneously and instantaneously, never separate or apart from each other, never looking for each other. Never do we have a person looking for a home; never do we have a landlord looking for a tenant.

"Never do we have a person seeking employment. Never do we have an employer seeking an employee. Always we have God appearing as employer and employee, but always simultaneously one. ... God appears as every individual necessary to the unfoldment of the idea, the presentation and the acceptance of the idea. ...

"The salesman goes out on his rounds during the day, performing the human functions of his job, but never does he go out and sell. He goes out only to perform the human functions of his job. The selling is done by God long before the salesman goes out upon his rounds. In fact, the salesman merely completes the transaction on paper, the transaction that was already complete in mind as the activity of mind. Once we begin to see God as individual being, we will then see why there is no need to go out and sell things to people. They come and buy them. It's a strange reversal of the human picture but a very true one."

Joel S. Goldsmith, "There Is No Law of Matter or Disease,"
The 1953 Los Angeles Practitioners' Class.

9

The Christ Kingdom

The principles of The Infinite Way are used to explain its purpose and function, but it is you and I who must embody these principles in order that they may come alive. What are the principles that we are to embody in our consciousness? What is the goal? Here is where The Infinite Way departs from concepts held by the rest of the world.

Certainly, it is true that I do not want to be bad, but neither do I want to be merely humanly good: I want to be spiritually pure. I do not want to be poor; I do not want to be rich: I want only God's spiritual grace. I do not want to be sick; I do not want to be well: I want God to be the health of my countenance; I want God's health, not mine. So when I am helping others, I must try to realize that I am not trying to make my patients well, employed, or pure: I am trying to bring the realization of God's qualities to them.

This goal is quite different from the goal of most persons when you realize within yourself that you are not trying to be healthy: you are trying to realize the health of God. You are not trying to be wealthy: you are trying to prove God's grace as your sufficiency—God's grace, not your wealth. You do not want to be bad, but you must be very careful that you do not think you are good because you will be setting yourself up as someone separate and apart from God. You seek only that God's good be expressed in and through you. You do not want to be miserly, but you do not want to be prodigal, either: you only want to be the instrument through which God's abundance is distributed.

In other words, no qualities are to be ascribed to you: not the bad or negative qualities and not the good or positive qualities. You strive to understand and always feel that it is God's love that flows through you, and then it is pure. You want God's life to flow as your life, and then it is immortal. You want God's grace to flow through you, and then it is abundant. Always it must be God's, never yours.

The Demonstration Is Always the Realization of Christhood

The healing of yourself and others becomes simple when you are not trying to change disease into health. What you are doing is trying to realize the nothingness of the mortal, whether it is a good mortal or a bad mortal, a healthy mortal or a sick mortal. You are trying to realize Christhood:

Christ, the Son of God, is my true identity. This is God's life, the Christ-life, that is being lived as me.

When you work this way, you are on The Infinite Way of demonstration. You are never demonstrating supply or health. Then what are you demonstrating? You are demonstrating the Christ. When you have that in your mind, whether the concern is with your problems, your family's, a patient's, or a student's, you will never forget that you are not trying to change disease into health, lack into abundance, or age into youth. You are only trying to realize the Christ, for the Christ, the son of God, is the life of man. Man has no other life but the God-life made manifest as individual life. You will not demonstrate supply: you will demonstrate God's grace, and that Grace is sufficient for every need.

God as the Only Power

When you conform to the Middle Path, not seeking to get rid of the evil or seeking to get the good, but always walking right down the middle, seeking only the realization of spiritual harmony, you are on the spiritual side, and you are living the principles of The Infinite Way which are valueless unless embodied. When you think of God's life, God's abundance, God's grace, or God's health as omnipotent, you can prove it; whereas if you think of sin, disease, lack, or age as something to be overcome, you will lose the way.

One of the most basic of all Infinite Way principles is that you do not use God as a power over discord, nor do you seek God for the purpose of getting rid of discord. Instead, you realize the allness of God and the nonpower of whatever the appearance may be.

Do not turn to God to win a victory or to overcome the sword or the bomb. "Put up again thy sword into his place: for they that take the sword shall perish with the sword."[1] Put up that use of power; stop the attempt to use a power; those who live by power will die by power. Turn to God in the realization of spiritual power as the infinite all, and then look out on the world of temporal powers as nonpower. You do not turn to God to persuade Him to do something or as if He were a power over evil. You, yourself, recognize the impotence of error.

Not Good People, but the
Presence of God Is Your Protection

When you are in a church, a temple, or any place where people have gathered for a spiritual purpose, you do not invoke God-power to protect yourself from anything or anybody there because unconsciously you think that you are in the presence of wholly good people. That is not true. Good people can turn to bad people very quickly, and even the very best people as measured by human standards can become harmful. If their security is jeopardized, they may do very strange things.

If you were trusting the persons in a certain place, resting contentedly and feeling safe from all harm because there are only good people there, you would be making a great mistake. You would be thinking of "man, whose breath is in his nostrils"[2] as being good, and suddenly he might rise up and prove how wrong you are. You can rest in any room in quietness and in confidence, however, if you carry with you the assurance that only God is present, only God is the Life of man, only God is the Soul of man. You can rest, not because of the people, but because of your realization of the presence of God.

If you go to any place of worship without turning to God for protection, because of the belief that the people there are all good, you are living in a fool's paradise. But if you are sitting there peacefully, quietly, joyously, without turning to God for protection, it could well be because you know that God constitutes man's being and God is good. Unless there is that realization when you leave the room, the church, or the temple, you would be reaching around for a God-power to protect you on the road or on the streets and you would be leaving behind you the kingdom of God. The moment you look for a God-power, you are acknowledging the presence of an evil power. But if you can walk out of any place that you consider a place of God in the assurance that God is the life of man and that man is on earth to show forth God's glory, you will then have entered into the healing consciousness of the Master.

You are in the kingdom of God only if you can stop searching for a God-power, if you can rest and not resist evil or call on God to protect you from evil. There is no power in evil. God constitutes individual being. God is the mind of man. The presence of God means the absence of evil. When you ascribe all-power and all-presence to God, you are not reaching out to use God as a power over error. Then, and only then, are you in the kingdom of God.

This is not easy for most persons because there is the belief that if only they could get God, they could use God as a club over evil. God is not a club to be used; God is not a sword to be used; God is not a power to be used. God is the very presence of individual being.

The Realized Presence of God Dissolves Fear

In healing work as practiced in The Infinite Way, the first thought that must come to your mind is that you are not turning to God to be a power over disease, sin, or lack. Your turning to God is in the realization that God alone is power and presence and there is no other power or presence on which to use God. One of the most difficult parts of The Infinite Way to teach and to understand is that God is not power in the sense of a power over something or over some condition. God is not a power over evil in any place. God is the only presence everywhere present.

There is hardly a person in all the world who does not fear. It is true that not everyone fears the same things, but practically every person knows fear of some kind. If there should be a few individuals who feel that there is nothing on earth that they fear, and I have not met one yet, somewhere in the back of their minds, there would still be the thought of the inevitability of death, and this would set up in them some fear. As a matter of fact, few persons would be concerned enough to want to cure disease if it were not for their belief that it might lead to death. Everyone wants to avoid death, and so he tries to get rid of his disease. Where there is no fear of death, even if there were disease, there would be no pain with it. Pain is our own resistance to the idea of death.

As long as you are in the earthly frame of consciousness, you will know some fear. If you can rise to Christ-consciousness, however, to the understanding that there are no evil powers, nothing to use God for or against, all fear disappears from your experience, even the fear of death.

God Is Not Overcoming: God Is Being

As long as there is a trace of belief in your mind that God can be used to overcome something, you are still in the old belief of two powers. When you come to the realization that God is the infinite All and there is nothing else, then you have come to an awareness of Infinite Way healing principles, where you do not heal anyone of disease, but where you realize that God's grace is omnipresent, and that what appears as sin, disease, death, lack, or limitation is but the human appearance, the belief in two powers.

In one way or another, come to the place where you do not reach out for God, but where you realize that God already is. If you reach out for God, you have some negative power that you want God to do something to. When you can relax in the realization, "Thank You, Father, Thou art.

Omnipotence is," you have nothing to get rid of, nothing to destroy. The negative appearance, the sick appearance, or the sinful appearance dissolves.

It is the reaching out for God to have God do something that is the barrier to spiritual demonstration. Instead, the way is relaxing and not reaching out to God for anything. Harmony already is; peace already is; joy already is; spirituality already is. You do not have to reach out to God to do something. Rest here and now in the realization that it is God's presence that ensures freedom, harmony, peace, contentment. With that awareness, you can walk up and down the street, ride up and down the road, and not reach out for God. Since you are not ascribing good or evil to man, you can sit back and relax in the assurance:

God's grace is here, and God's grace is my sufficiency, my protection in all things.

The Indwelling Spirit of God

As you think of all those who are a part of your experience, remember that there is a Spirit in man. Instead of looking on the frame which you see—the form or the figure—look through it and realize that the spirit of God is in every man and woman you are seeing. How different they look when you see them in that light, instead of just as a man or a woman. Now they are not merely a man or woman: they are man and woman plus the spirit of God that dwells not only in them but in the consciousness of everyone. There is a Spirit moving in and through every person who is a part of your consciousness, and this Spirit is your supply and their supply, health, abundance, and integrity.

I have the spirit of God in me, the source of my health and strength, the source of my supply, the source of whatever integrity I may show forth. The Spirit in me is the source of my entire life.

This Spirit has not been left out of anybody. The spirit of God indwells you, and It is the resurrection of your life. It can overcome the lost years of the locust. If your temple has been destroyed, in three days It can raise up the temple of your body, your health, your business, your home, or your family; It can resurrect out of any grave any part of your experience by your acknowledgment that His Spirit dwells in you.

In spite of any appearance to the contrary, the indwelling Spirit is here, everywhere present in everyone, even in hospitals and prisons. The spirit of God is in everyone in the government. That is hard to realize sometimes, but it must be done. With this realization, you have no evils to overcome. You have nothing to do because the spirit of God that dwells in you does the work. The responsibility is off your shoulders.

You have to realize that this same Spirit indwells every member of your household even though some seem to be trying to prove that they are children of the devil. It is like some youngsters who try to convince you that they are bad or indifferent. It is not true; it is a human trait based on the misunderstanding of their true identity. All that can be changed by knowing the truth. "The Spirit of the Lord God is upon me.[3]... I can do all things through Christ which strengtheneth me.[4] ... He that raised up Christ from the dead shall also quicken your mortal bodies by his Spirit that dwelleth in you."[5]

But that is not enough unless you have seen this Spirit indwelling. When you live with this passage of the indwelling

Spirit, you will eventually feel It within you as if It were a living presence. It is a living presence, and It is within you, but you have neglected to tabernacle or commune with It. Communion has nothing to do with an outside experience: it has to do with an inner experience. You commune with the Spirit that indwells you by shutting out the world when you are in your inner sanctuary, realizing the closeness of the spirit of God, this power of grace and resurrection.

Realization and Not Mere Words

In The Infinite Way, passages of the Bible are used to gain from them the principles that they are meant to convey. Reciting the statement, "My grace is sufficient for thee,"[6] will never bring sufficiency to you, but understanding that idea and gaining a realization that there is within you a presence and power of Grace helps you rely, not on the statement, but on the inner Grace. This makes the difference. Often the statement, "I believe in God," is made, or "I have faith in God," and all this can be a barrier to God's help. When you have gone beyond belief and beyond faith to the realization that God is the very being of your being, when you have understood that God is the very life of your life, you are not believing in God any more; you are not having faith in God any more: you are communing with God within yourself, not merely having a belief or a faith in God.

You can never rest or be satisfied with a statement of truth until you come to the actual experience of that statement. There must be the experience that God's grace is your sufficiency. You have to experience the fact that you are on earth as the instrument through which God's glory is made evident. It is not enough to think or declare it. There must come a moment of experience when you can say, "I have no life of my own. I did not make this life. This life is God's very own life, breathed and expressed as me." When you have that experience, it is an actual communion with that Life which animates you.

Working with Bible Passages Brings the Experience of Oneness

Every scripture in the world reveals that within your own being there is an *I or a Me;* there is a Presence, a Power. As students of spiritual wisdom you will begin to work with Bible passages so that every time a problem confronts you, you are able to say to yourself, "He that is within me is greater than any problem in the world or any person in the world," or "He performeth the thing that is appointed for me,"[7] or "The Lord will perfect that which concerneth me."[8] The more you live with the idea that there is a He that is right where you are and that Its function in your life is to be the power of resurrection or redemption, or the power of Grace, your consciousness changes from one of fear, doubt, or lack of confidence into one of absolute assurance that even if you of your own self cannot do it, there is a Presence that can and does. Relaxing into that, you bring it about.

Living and dwelling with every Bible passage of spiritual import brings the ability to experience it. The teaching is: "I and my Father are one.[9]... Son, thou art ever with me, and all that I have is thine."[10] But always there is the temptation of twoness. There is God somewhere, but then there is a "me" over here. And where is God in this moment of trouble? Because of the picture of twoness, it becomes necessary to return over and over again to the realization, "Ah, but

I and my Father are really one. I am not separated from my Father. If I make my bed in hell, I and the Father are one. If 'I walk through the valley of the shadow of death,'[11]... I and my Father are one.'" When you hear, "Son, thou art ever with me, and all that I have is thine," there is a relaxing.

Working with a passage of that kind over a period of time brings the actual experience of oneness and a continuous inner assurance: "All that I have is thine." It breaks the spell of looking outside as if you were waiting for something to come to you, or as if there were something you needed. Every time you turn from the appearance that you are here and God is somewhere else to the assurance, "I and the Father are one. Here where I am, God is," you are communing with the truth within and it leads to an experience where all of a sudden it comes: "'Whereas I was blind, now I see.'[12] Whereas before I knew it with words, now I feel it. I have the actual experience of God's presence."

All the principles which are based on scriptural passages must be practiced and lived with until the experience takes place. As long as truth is in the realm of words, whether words in the Bible or words of a teacher, you have not entered the kingdom of God. You enter the kingdom of spiritual awareness only when a certain movement or transition in consciousness takes place.

All the Bible passages and all the principles of The Infinite Way constitute the letter of truth, but the letter of truth itself kills. Just to recite or memorize them is not life eternal; it is not the bread of life. It is only when you live with them until they translate themselves into an experience that they are living waters, the bread and the wine of inspiration.

Keep Truth Active in Consciousness

What takes place within you consciously is what you demonstrate. You must know the truth if you are to be made free of the discords of the world, of its temptations, sins, unhappiness, and diseases. Consciously know that the spirit of God in you is the peace wherever you go, and the spirit of God in every individual you meet is the peace unto every situation. "My peace I give unto you."[13] The peace that is the spirit of God in the midst of you, this is the peace that is given unto you. Christ-peace, the Son-of-God peace, is at the center of your being, but it is also at the center of everyone's being. Wherever you go, raise it up.

Christ must be raised from the tomb of the mortal self. You must raise It up by consciously knowing that the Christ in the midst of you is the source of peace, power, dominion, freedom, joy, health, and abundance. Then you must raise up that Christ out of the tomb of every human being you meet. Raise up the Christ by looking right into the person and saying, "Ah, I have been judging you by your outer appearance instead of realizing that the same spirit of God that dwells in me and is my peace dwells in you and is the presence of peace."

The whole activity of The Infinite Way is an activity of your consciousness. It is an activity of consciousness that must be attained by knowing the truth. Then you can enjoy the peace that you feel at this moment, and it can be permanent because you realize it is God's peace, not man's peace; it is God's grace, not man's will to be good. As you go about your work, you will know that the peace of this world is not dependent on man's being good or man's being bad: it is dependent on God in the midst of man. What has destroyed man has been believing that there were good men and bad men, always hoping for good men, and not finding enough of them. That will all end when you are not interested in whether man is good or bad.

God's grace is my sufficiency, and God's grace is the sufficiency of this world. Why should I fear "man, whose breath is in his nostrils"? God's grace is peace; God's grace is life; God's grace is health; God's grace is wholeness.

The Activity of Truth Brings Freedom

There are too many students who read Infinite Way books and hear the message, but do not practice it. They then wonder why peace does not come to them. They are looking for a God somewhere, when it is their knowing the truth that makes them free. They are waiting for some Christ to come and do something, when it is knowing the Christ of their own being that brings harmony into their life.

This is not an activity of blind faith, of sitting around dull and dead, listening to somebody preach, and then because they are preaching, hoping that God is going to do something. This is a teaching of the spiritual nature of your own being when you know the truth. It is not that your nature is not spiritual when you are not knowing it. It is that *that* spirituality is not in evidence.

The activity of truth in consciousness is not trying to make bad men good, nor is it trying to get anything from reasonable men. It is an activity of knowing:

My dependence is on the Christ of God in the midst of man. I seek my security and my safety, not by the will of man, but by the will of God; not by the grace of man, but by the grace of God; not by appealing to the reasonableness of man, but by realizing the omnipotence and omnipresence of God.

I am seeking my good spiritually, not humanly. I am seeking my safety and security spiritually, not through temporal means, not even by means of man's good nature, reasonableness, or sanity.

Do not put your life, your safety, or your security in the hands of men, no matter who those men may be, nor in any combination of governments, no matter what it may be. If you had to make your safety dependent on somebody's sanity, you would be risking everything you have if the person turned out to be insane. Your safety, your security, and your peace must come forth from the Christ of God which is in the midst of man, and your recognition of this is what brings it into being. When you place your whole life and being—your health, wealth, and harmony—in the Christ of your being, you will have it forever. No man will take it from you.

Let the world alone to awaken to its own way, but remember those who live by might and power are not going to save the world, whether they build bombs or refrain from doing so. The world will be saved by the recognition and the realization of the Christ in the midst of you. The Christ is not a temporal power. Christ Jesus came as a spiritual power. He preached a kingdom not of this world, not an earthly kingdom, but a kingdom where there is neither good nor evil but only spiritual perfection. The mission of the Christ is to reveal the kingdom of God on earth and then all that is unlike the kingdom of God will eventually dissolve and disappear.

The Christ is a spiritual kingdom; the Christ is a spiritual power. Do not think of It in terms of Its fighting the world, yet the world will dissolve in the presence of the Christ.

Across the Desk

Every serious Infinite Way student must accept the responsibility to practice and live Infinite Way principles. If the telephone rings with a plea for help or if we hear or see some disturbing situation or person, we must look upon it as an appeal to the Christ of our being and immediately reinterpret the picture being presented to us. Our practice must not be limited only to the problems of human experience, but every harmonious human picture is also a call upon us to reinterpret it, recognizing the source of all good and that there is no good or evil in form or effect. Whatever of good we are seeing is more of God shining through.

As we diligently practice the principles of The Infinite Way, we become aware of something very important taking place within. A moment comes when these principles take over our life and live as us. Our job, hour after hour, is to keep ourselves open to the flow from within and thereby be instruments for the effortless and joyous activity of God.

Tape Recorded Excerpts
Prepared by the Editor

Many persons have strange concepts of what living the spiritual life involves. They believe it causes a person to violate every intelligent rule of living and makes him eccentric, unbalanced, and incapable of living a normal life. Perhaps the following excerpts will help to clarify and dissipate any such misconception.

Normalcy in Living

"God is the life of our being; God is the soul of our being. Nowhere in our experience will this give us liberty to violate what we call natural law or commonsense, but rather to bring these laws into harmonious expression in our individual life. In other words, because we say that Jesus ignored the Commandments, 'Thou shalt not steal,' and 'Thou shalt not commit adultery,' it does not mean that we have license to steal and commit adultery. No, it means that as we attain the realization that God is our mind and our life, any need for or desire for theft or adultery passes out of our experience.

"It does not mean that because Jesus ignored the Commandment, 'Honor thy father and thy mother,' that we will have the privilege of ignoring our father and mother, but rather that in attaining to his command of 'Love thy neighbor as thyself,' we have attained the realization of the care of our parents, our children, or our neighbor. ... It is that very love that we have for our neighbor that enables us to fulfill our destiny as Christ-being. Any falling away from an activity of love would be a falling away from our true spiritual nature.

"In the same way when we speak of God as the one Power and agree that nothing besides Him is power, we do not mean that it would be wisdom to go out and drink bottles of poison just to prove that it has not power or that we would ignore our daily... common sense eating habits, drinking habits, clothing habits, exercise habits. When we exercise for health and strength, we make a mistake. When we exercise as a normal part of our daily activity, and eat sensibly and intelligently and cleanly as a part of our daily living, then we are fulfilling at least one part of spiritual law which is normalcy in all things. ...

"We should have no feeling that in turning wholeheartedly, devotedly, completely to the Spirit as the Source of our existence, we are turning away from the practicality of intelligence in the ordinary affairs of daily living, or that we will be compelled to give up our practical politics or practical statesmanship, practical business activities, or practical building activities. No, no. It is true that some people will eventually have to give up the activity of the sale of alcoholic liquors or playing around with inventing more destructive forms of weapons. Those things do not come into harmony with the Spirit."

Joel S. Goldsmith, "Transcendental."
The 1952 Honolulu Closed Class.

"Someone in the office may come in some morning and announce having been ill all night. ... You answer him in his own language. ... When he announces that he is ill it is just nice to say, 'That's too bad, but I know that it will pass quickly,' and anything else that the Father puts on the lips to say, but never, never, never let us lose this common touch. Never let us lose the touch with our fellow man. Remember that in the 25ᵗʰ Chapter of Matthew, if your fellow man is in prison, go there and visit him. If your fellow man is sick, speak of health to him in his own language even while internally you are voicing it in the language of the Spirit as you understand it. If your neighbor is in a hospital, do not hesitate to go there and visit him and bring flowers to him, too, and if he feels he needs a bottle of vitamin pills, let him have that, too. Let us meet our brothers' need not on our level of what we believe they need, but on what they at the moment believe they need.

"You might as well mark this down, too: if I should at any time ask you for help, please don't throw me any metaphysical cliches. Do not tell me it isn't true and that it doesn't hurt because I am apt to get very mad. All I ask when I ask for help is that you say, 'Yes, I'll give it,' and then sit back and whatever God gives you in realization have it secretly and silently, and I will feel it openly. I get awfully antagonistic when people hand me these ready-made cliches that they haven't yet attained because if they had I would be feeling the effects of it before they could voice it."

Joel S. Goldsmith, "Principles of Spiritual Living,"
The 1954 Third New York Practitioners' Class.

"In our ordinary human existence, it is perfectly normal and natural if we are talking about a candidate for office to speak of the good human qualities of one as against the qualities, good or bad, of another. In other words, we may review an individual's life and prefer one to another as president, governor, or mayor. If one is employing help, one would look at his qualifications and select the one best qualified for that particular position, thinking of his qualifications in terms of education and experience.

"That is quite a different thing than when we come to our contemplation of God and the realization of God as man's true being. When in our relationships with this world we are considering the [activities] of living... going marketing, shopping, out in the bus, or down here to this hotel, we are faced with humanity at many levels: some good, some bad, and some intolerable. There is no point in not recognizing that as a matter of humanity, humanity is graded. But even while noting that in the outer, can you see how wrong that would be if, really and truly within, you did not have the feeling of 'Father, forgive them.' They are not good humans or bad humans: they are really spiritual being, children of God. It is true that they are not awake to it. That is what makes them of differing degrees of humanity: the degree of their non-awakeness to the truth of their being. ...They have no reason to believe there is a God. They are living a human life that is just about as hopeless as can be: debt, high taxes, lack of savings, everything in this human world facing them and no hope. ...

"Wherever we behold with our eyes these differing degrees of humanhood, and even while in our business experience we have to make use of it in employing help or being employed... and in our selection of governmental officers, nevertheless keep your major measuring rod within yourself to realize that regardless of appearances, good or bad, the real nature of man is God."

Joel S. Goldsmith, "All Things Work Together for Good."
The 1954 Chicago Closed Class.

* 10 *

REJECTING APPEARANCES
AND CONCEPTS

IT WAS NOT easy for the followers of the Masters to be told, "My kingdom is not of this world." The only world they knew was the world of Roman domination, the world of the synagogue and the temple, the world of the farm and trade. There was no hint in their teaching that there was any other world except the one to be found after death. That there could be another world, another kingdom here and now, was entirely outside the belief of the human being who lived out from the pairs of opposites.

Jesus tried in many different ways to let his followers know about this kingdom. When he spoke of a bread and a meat the world knows not, he was speaking of the bread of a different kingdom, an entirely different consciousness. He spoke of living waters and the many mansions in the Father's house.

Most of the Hebrews knew nothing about mansions. Most of them were hard workers and yet he told them, "In my Father's house are many mansions: if it were not so, I would have told you. I go to prepare a place for you."[1] Where was that place? What did he mean? They were expecting Jesus to go to Jerusalem and overthrow not only the temple but Rome as well: They were expecting that he would overthrow one temporal kingdom and present them with another temporal government. But when he got there, he did not do any overthrowing.

It is not too different today when on the one hand there are people who are trying to overthrow the temporal kingdom of communism, and, on the other hand, the communists are trying to overcome or overthrow the temporal kingdom of capitalism, both of them hoping to replace the form they oppose with some form they consider better. That is about as high as the human mind can reach: a better temporal kingdom or a healthier body.

Man's Expansion into
Outer Space Broke Limitations

It is hard for a human being to go higher in consciousness than to think in terms other than that of a healthy body instead of a sick one, a young one instead of an old one, an active one instead of an inactive one. He is always thinking in terms of what he already knows, because he lacks the capacity to believe that there is something beyond what he knows.

Only within the last few years has man grasped the idea of exploring outer space, and with that exploration has discovered that it is possible to go into even an earthly realm beyond the one by which he has been limited, just as he had been limited by the horizon before 1492. That limitation was broken. Another limitation, that of crossing a continent on horseback or with a horse and carriage, was also broken. Limitation after limitation has been broken down but always in the temporal realm.

A New Dimension

Those who caught glimpses of the kingdom about which the Master was speaking have always tried to tell us of a spiritual state of consciousness in which there are different values, even different forms. As we entered the metaphysical age, the emphasis became that of changing one temporal form for another: the form of disease for the form of health, the form of lack for the form of abundance, the form of loneliness for the form of companionship, the form of homelessness for the form of home, or the form of unemployment for the form of employment. It was all centered on the world of effect, merely trying to attain a better effect or more of some particular effect.

In a mystical teaching, we try to lift ourselves into another consciousness, the fourth dimensional or spiritual consciousness, so that we can begin to behold the mansions the Father has prepared for us. The Christ-consciousness goes before our human self and then lifts our human self above itself.

Not Good Humanhood but Spiritual Reality

When we quote, quite glibly at times, "My kingdom is not of this world.[2]... I have meat to eat that ye know not of.[3]... I am the bread of life,"[4] have we even the faintest idea of the meaning of those statements or do we think that they refer to a temporal kingdom? Are we trying to take a spiritual teaching and bring it down to the level of our human experience instead of dying daily to the human experience in order that we may be reborn of the Spirit? Unless there is a dying to the human sense of things, there cannot be a rebirth into spiritual reality.

There is a spiritual kingdom, but no one will ever see it while his mind is intent merely on exchanging a bad material condition for a good one. No one will ever behold the spiritual kingdom until he learns that all human experience, both the discordant appearance and the harmonious appearance, is an illusion of the five senses. In *The Infinite Way*[5] there are many passages stating that health is as much of an illusion as sickness and that we must rise above the belief of health the same as we rise above the belief of disease.

We have to rise even above the belief of life just as we have to rise above the belief of death because life and death in the human sense are just opposite ends of the same stick. They both have a beginning and an ending. As long as we are thinking in terms of preventing death in order to have life, it means that even if we succeeded we are merely postponing death. It is only when we stop thinking in terms of life and in terms of death and begin to think in terms of our immortal, eternal, incorporeal being that we will discover that life which is life eternal.

No one enters the kingdom of God by being merely a healthy human being or even by being a good human being. The Master clarified that for us for all time when he said, "Except your righteousness shall exceed the righteousness of the scribes and Pharisees, ye shall in no case enter into the kingdom of heaven."[6] There was nobody more righteous than they. Again Jesus emphasized the unimportance of human good in attaining spiritual realization when he said, "Among them that are born of women there hath not risen a greater than John the Baptist: notwithstanding he that is least in the kingdom of heaven is greater than he."[7]

To reach the spiritual realization of being, it is necessary that our thought ascend above trying to change human conditions and that we begin to have a real longing to know God.

Becoming Aware of Spiritual Reality

One of the most difficult concepts for almost every student of The Infinite Way is to understand what is meant by beholding God. There are nature mystics in the world who believe that God is in nature, that God is manifested in the sun, moon, and stars, in the flowers and the plants, but the truth is that what we behold with the five physical senses is nothing more nor less than a creation of the universal human mind. It is in no way divine or spiritual: it is only our limited concept of the spiritual.

If God were in a tree, a tree would not die; if God were in the ocean, there would not be a storm on it. How long ago was it known that God is not in the whirlwind, that God is not in the storm, that God is not in any phenomena of nature! These represent the creation of the Lord God or mind as set forth in the second chapter of Genesis. It is only when we see the sun, moon, stars, rivers, vegetables, and all nature as symbols, or as the human concept of the real, that we begin to perceive that behind this creation there is *My* kingdom, a temple not made with hands. "God that made the world and all things therein, seeing that he is Lord of heaven and earth, dwelleth not in temples made with hands."[8]

Once we perceive that there is a spiritual kingdom not made with hands, eternal in the heavens, we will then know the consciousness into which we must be lifted before we can behold reality. While we are merely trying to change the human picture, even succeeding in making it a very pleasant one temporarily, we have not yet touched the spiritual realm. The Master would never have given the world this teaching had he not received it from within. The lives of the mystics have shown us that what Jesus said was true and that some of them perceived it in a small measure and some in great measure.

The Impermanence of Human Good

Is it not absurd to make ourselves perfectly healthy today, knowing all the time that a germ, some wrong food, an accident, a bomb, or a bullet could destroy it all? Does it now show what folly it is to spend a lifetime trying to get a healthy body or a few extra dollars when almost anything in this universe can upset it in an instant? While I am not belittling the joys and benefits of abundant health and abundant supply, our time can better be spent in bringing forth the spiritual awareness of health and supply, permanent and eternal, not made with human thoughts but a health and supply that are divine.

From the very beginning, the major vision of The Infinite Way has been not to treat disease to get rid of sickness and get health or to take human footsteps to gain supply, but to rise to another dimension of life. These ideas, together with that of incorporeality, have given us in plain ABC's, not only what the vision is but how to attain it. What our daily practice must be and how we are to train ourselves when these appearances are brought forcibly to our attention is thoroughly explained in "Contemplation Develops the Beholder" in *The Contemplative Life*[9] and in "Living above the Pairs of Opposites" in *A Parenthesis in Eternity*.[10] In traditional metaphysics the reality of evil was denied, but no one is really in The Infinite Way until he is not only recognizing the unreality of the evil appearance but also the unreality of the good appearance. In other words, good weather must be seen as but the opposite of bad weather, both of them physical phenomena and therefore not of the nature of reality. So, too, we must look upon physical health, not as if a person had accomplished something great in attaining it, but actually that it is as much of an illusion as ill health.

The Goal, a God-Governed World

With spiritual vision and the understanding of the real nature of God's universe, we will have a world of people here on earth God-governed. The Master told us that as in heaven so on earth God's government would reign, and God's government is not sin or disease or war or death. This world that we would enjoy through spiritual consciousness would be a world of harmony but not the harmony of today and the discord of tomorrow. It would be the harmony of God which is eternal; it would be the life of God which is eternal. There would not be four billion people, each believing he has a life of his own.

If we begin with the smallest problem that comes to our attention and if we hold faithfully to the truth of a spiritual universe, we will rise above it. As we are willing to undertake greater problems, more vital and more serious ones, gradually we will overcome them, too, through our spiritual awareness. If the Wright brothers could fly fifty-seven seconds, we can understand why we can fly a thousand miles an hour. But first they had to fly fifty-seven seconds. Some of us can remember when Bleriot received five thousand pounds for flying twenty-six miles across the English Channel. Now we don't even get paid for a three thousand mile flight across the Atlantic Ocean. In the short span of a lifetime we have gone from thinking of a twenty-six mile flight as something very unusual to thinking of a three thousand mile flight as just a part of the day's livelihood for a pilot.

Healing, the Result of Knowing the
Unreal Nature of Appearances

In spiritual work it sometimes seems almost impossible to help a person with his problem because there is that feeling of not knowing how, of not having the power. Gradually we learn that healing is not brought about by power: healing is brought about by our awareness of the unreal nature of appearances—not only of discordant appearances but of harmonious ones. That is the essence of the spiritual healing principle.

The healing principle is not bringing God-power into the world; it is not the power given to one person only who has been especially chosen to heal the sick. Whatever God does for one, God does for all. It is a question of whether a person is willing to pay the price, and in spiritual healing one price is the ability to control the emotions so that he does not react to appearances, so that he does not become shocked at the most horrible appearances and does not glory too much in the health that he sees restored.

In The Infinite Way we accept healing as the natural result of our understanding, just as an architect builds and designs a house and knows that the completed structure is the product of his understanding of architectural laws. A pilot pilots a plane, but he does not go around looking for medals every day. He knows that being able to maneuver a large plane is the natural result of his understanding of the principles underlying aerodynamics.

So it is that spiritual healing is the direct result or fruitage of our ability not to respond emotionally to the appearance-world, realizing that if we can see it, hear it, taste it, touch it, or smell it, it is not of God. Therefore we dismiss it. We do not try to improve, heal, change, or enrich it, but we dismiss it in the understanding that there is a spiritual kingdom which is the reality. This kingdom is not observable to the finite senses.

Only in our awakened spiritual consciousness do we know that there is a spiritual kingdom right here on earth. We do not go any place to find those many mansions; we do not go any place to find "My kingdom." Why? Because that kingdom is in no other place than within us. What we realize in our consciousness becomes evident in the experience of all those who touch it and even many who never know that we are on earth.

Nonreaction Is All-Important

How many times in the writings is it brought to our attention that it is our reaction to the appearance that determines the outer circumstance. We are dealing not with conditions but with mental concepts, and when they hit up against the truth, the concepts dissolve and disappear just as light coming into the room dissolves darkness, yet the light does not dissolve the darkness because there is no such thing as darkness.

To God the dark and the light are the same. Anything of a physical nature, whether it is negative or positive, evil or good, is the same in the eyes of God: illusion or nothingness. When both ends of the stick are recognized by us as being unreal, then we can say the same thing. Sickness and physical health, darkness and light, sin and purity are one and the same. They are all mortal illusion, all nothingness, the dream. Our recognition of that brings about what in human language is called healing, and then somebody says, "I feel better" or "I've had a healing." It is not that an evil condition has been changed to a good one: it is that the entire material scene is dissolved and spiritual harmony has been brought to light.

In the Master's teaching much stress is placed on the word *I*: "I will never leave thee.[11]... I am with you alway, even unto the end of the world.[12] ... I am the bread of life.[13]... I am the resurrection and the life."[14] Jesus is always trying to bring to our attention the truth that the reality, the substance, is within us, and not outside to be attained. The appearance-world would say that our good is external to us and must be attained, but Spirit reveals:

Whatever I am seeking, I am. All that the Father has is mine. The I of my being is the source of my existence.

Then why react to this outer human scene? Why react to the evil appearance or the good appearance when through inner vision our task is to perceive that the secret of life is within?

The Fatherhood of God Inevitably Leads to the Brotherhood of Man

The secret of life is in the *I* that I am which is the *I* that you are. The one *I* unites us in a spiritual bond so that we are of one household, of one Father. "Call no man your father upon the earth: for one is your Father, which is in heaven."[15] The moment that we accept the mental concept of this world, the mind-picture, it would be ludicrous to believe that we all have one Father because we may always have lived thousands of miles apart, and my father never was where you were. My father is white, and somebody else's father is black. How impossible it is to try to translate truth into human terms!

There is a way, however, for each one of us spiritually to discern the truth that our human parents are not really the creators of our life, but that the creative Principle of life antedates our parents, grandparents, great grandparents. This creative Principle of life is one, and that one is Spirit. All else is an emanation of that Spirit. Therefore, there is but one Father, and because there is but one Father we are of one spiritual household, united in a spiritual bond.

The teaching of the fatherhood of God and the brotherhood of man has always been known to the mystics, and when we begin to live out from that standpoint we will not try to prevent children from being born and we will not have to kill off those who are here through war and famine. There will be an abundance on earth for us to share with all those who do not have, and what we share will be multiplied over and over again. We do not multiply by withholding. We multiply by outpouring.

Our vision is not on changing evil to good but having seen the evil and the good as human, mortal, carnal illusion, our attitude then is:

Reveal to me spiritual reality. Reveal to me Thy grace as my sufficiency— not health as my sufficiency, nor abundance, but Thy grace.

Grace reveals to us our spiritual Selfhood. In Infinite Way writings there are hundreds of references to the truth that there is but one Selfhood, and it is spiritual. That is a denial of appearances when there seem to be thousands of us. But regardless of how we may appear or who we may appear to be, there is only one Selfhood, the spiritual Selfhood which I am and you are and which is the embodiment of our good. In this truth lies the eternality of our existence, the incorporeal, spiritual existence which we are, co-existent with God since before the beginning of time.

In Order to Know God, Be Still

An English poet once said, "Before God was, I am." We have existed even before there was a concept of God, even before anyone thought it necessary to look around for a supernatural something to do something for us, who are already incorporeal, spiritual, perfect, harmonious, and eternal. Do you not see that only in humanhood do people have to invent God? The God to whom people are praying is a man-made God, an image of their thought, a human concept, and they are expecting this human concept to do something. No wonder all the billions of prayers that have gone up to God to restore somebody's health are not answered. Man has invented superpowers to do something for him that has already been done, that is already his natural state of being.

We do not have to pray to some kind of a super-God: we stand still when an appearance presents itself and say, "I cannot accept it because it is not of God," and then witness harmony appearing.

There is God, but to be aware of God it becomes necessary for the mind to be still, for us to be receptive and responsive, and then let that which is God reveal Itself. Begging is not going to do it; pleading is not going to do it; nor will tithing or bribery. The only way to know God is to be still. "Be still, and know that I am God."[16] Be still. Be still. Let God reveal Itself, and then let us listen until we hear: "The kingdom of God is within us," and that is where it has to be discovered and that is where it has to reveal itself. If we do not find it at first seeking, we have to go back again and again, deeper and deeper until it is reached.

The spiritual wisdom that has come down to us through all the ages has come from within the consciousness of those mystics who are attuned to receive it. The attunement comes by the ability to have periods of inner listening, contemplation, meditation, and quiet, whatever it is that will enable a person to be so still that the voice can come through and be heard. Whether It is heard audibly or merely sensed is not important. The important thing is that something comes through from within.

The periods of quiet and the periods of meditation can be short but they must be frequent because in these meditations a vacuum must take place, an expectancy for something that we know not—not something we know but something we know not—something beyond our ability to know, so that when it comes, it can come with a message that would startle the world but for which we have prepared ourselves by the very act of meditation.

How Great Is Our Capacity to Receive?

Nothing will come through of any nature beyond our ability to grasp because the degree of our capacity to receive determines what can come through, probably in the same way that a one inch water pipe will not admit anything more than one inch of water. Our capacity to receive determines the depth of the message we receive. As our capacity grows so do the depth, the richness, and the rightness of the message grow. That is why the greater the mystic the greater spiritual wisdom that is brought to earth. Whether or not we have any desire to bring through the greater wisdom is of no importance. As a matter of fact I do not believe anyone can have such a desire. The desire can only be:

Instruct me in so far as I can receive instruction today, and show me how to utilize whatever is given me.

One grain of truth at a time is enough because it multiplies itself. What we read in the books, however, serves as the inspiration that takes us back within ourselves and enables us then to receive from the same Source from which the mystics received. To develop our own capacity for greater awareness is far more important than anything else can ever be. From this comes the illumination that ultimately can save a world that cannot be saved any other way. There is too much destructive power on earth today to believe for a moment that the world can be saved unless man's spiritual nature comes through and brings with it the wisdom of the ages and a universal love.

ACROSS THE DESK

"And the government shall be upon His shoulders" was the prophecy of Isaiah. Herein lies the inescapable principle for all dedicated Infinite Way students to practice daily in order that this great prophecy of Isaiah may be fulfilled. With all the adverse news about government pressing in upon us, we do not side-step our responsibility to bring this principle forth in national and international affairs.

God, the Father, reveals Himself as God, the Son, in active expression. The activity of that one Father appearing as the Son is in reality the only government in operation. The practice of this principle leads to greater insight in choosing to public office those who represent integrity and intelligence which in turn will express as better government here and now.

TAPE RECORDED EXCERPTS
Prepared by the Editor

One of the responsibilities every citizen must accept is exercising his franchise to vote. This should not be based on individual prejudices or inherited party affiliations, but on carefully examining the qualifications of a candidate. However, then The Infinite Way student must take another step and that is to turn within in meditation for further light and guidance with the attitude: "Father, show me whom Thou hast chosen."

Accepting the
Responsibilities of Citizenship

"You and I, as citizens of a country, must fulfill our obligations as citizens. ... If the ignorance of our governmental leaders should get us into wars, as that same ignorance has done in every previous war, then also as citizens, we have functions to perform. We have to 'render unto Caesar the things that are Caesar's.' We can't run and hide our head and say, 'I will not fulfill my duty as a citizen, but I'll let you, my neighbor, go out and do it for me.' No, in whatever way is necessary, we are called upon to accept our responsibilities as citizens. ...

"Even while we are rendering 'unto Caesar the things that are Caesar's,'... we can be about our special business of prayer, of bringing the realization of the kingdom of God to earth through our consciousness. We can be helping to settle the affairs of the world, not by might and not by power, but by the spirit of God, so that... we can be a bigger power than the man who built the atomic bomb. ...

"None of us has any idea who may be reached by the Christ and... be in a position behind the affairs of the world where his influence can throw the situation to the side of spiritual power. It is for this reason that even if we comment on the qualities of this one, that one, or the other one, we do not in the same breath condemn, for it may be that very one who may have the awakening. ...

"It is not a person who is going to save the world. It is not a person who is going to come forth with an idea. It is the Christ, and the individual in the right place, at the right time, with a degree of receptivity will be the individual through whom It will appear to come. But you and I do not have to judge or appoint him. You and I do not even have to wonder who he is, or where. We need only dwell in the realization that salvation will come, not by might, nor by power, but by the spirit of God. Your function and mine is to be an instrument through which the presence of God can touch humanity. That is our only reason for living. ...

"Students of The Infinite Way around this globe must accept the responsibility for the world conditions of today. It has been said, and I'm sure rightly said, that you are getting the kind of government you deserve, and everyone does. Sometimes that is hard to believe, but it's true. ... The vast majority of the citizens of any country are responsible for the type of government they have, and when they don't want it, it won't be that way. ... We don't need majorities. 'One with God is a majority.' ... We have no way of knowing the degree of power there is in one individual consciously realizing the presence of God.

"Our faith is not in might or in power; our real faith isn't in the ballot either, because that's merely the might of numbers or percentages. Our ultimate reliance is in the degree of our aware-ness of the presence of God, in the degree of our realization of the impersonal nature of the Christ as being the seat of govern-ment, not 'man, whose breath is in his nostrils.' Therefore, let us accept the responsibility, and I don't mean that English people should accept the responsibility for the government of England and Americans should accept the responsibility for the govern-ment of America. That is stupidity; that is drawing a line about mine and thine. ...

"Anything that takes place in Australia can affect those in

England and affect us even more so in Hawaii. So let us not be concerned only about the governments of England, Ireland, Wales, or South Africa, but of the world, of the spiritual kingdom being humanly manifest."

Joel S. Goldsmith, "Grace,"
The 1958 London Advanced Class.

"Every man who has betrayed anyone or anything was first put in a position to do the betraying. You and I have never betrayed a nation, but nobody ever gave us the reins of authority. You first must empower someone before he can betray the power. ... Shall I have faith that there is a man or group of men who can save me individually or the world collectively? ...

"A very small group of individuals who no longer place their confidence in a political party or political candidate can change the entire result of an election. ... That does not mean they can elect their candidate or their party. It only means that out of the candidates who are running, those nearest to the level of spiritual integrity will be elected. That would be done only by those who could give up their faith and confidence in any man or party and realize that no power is in the visible.

"In certain places, votes are controlled by certain interests. For example, in some places it could be said that the labor vote will control the election in that community; in some other community it could be said that a church would dominate the election because [their members] are in the majority, and they would control the election; in some other places it would be said that the industrialists have control of the votes in their community and would do it. It is that very belief that perpetuates the evils of our political world because the power is not in an individual or in a group. The power is in the Spirit, and when we withdraw our faith, hope, confidence, or fear and place our entire reliance on the Invisible, 'there is always some leveling circumstances that puts down the overbearing. ... Though no checks to a new evil appear, the checks exist, and will appear. ... The dice of God are always loaded.' The leveling circumstance is God, spiritual law."

Joel S. Goldsmith, "The Dice of God Are Loaded—Emerson,"
The 1960 Hawaiian Village Open Class.

"You pray for guidance as to whom to vote for. You will go to the polls on election day and you'll vote. You'll find no excuse to stay home. And you do that as an obligation of citizenship. But you won't expect that the world's problems are going to be solved that way. The world's problems are going to be solved spiritually. ... As citizens we will vote for whoever it is that is revealed to us within ourselves as being the highest human form of government. But heaven forbid that we should put the responsibility on any President, Governor, Senator, or Congressman to save the world when we are in a spiritual dynasty, where we know that the government is on His shoulder.

"We have the opportunity to witness our lives so spiritually governed that the discords of this world will not come nigh our dwelling place. ... While there is an opportunity for us to be governed by good administrations in the capitals of the world, while there is the possibility of our enjoying good incomes just because times are good and business is good, as long as there is an opportunity to enjoy good health because we are within the age bracket where good health is the most usual thing, we do not find it easy to accept our opportunity for spiritual health, spiritual supply, spiritual government, nor to place our entire hope, confidence, faith, and reliance in the spiritual means.

"But now, we are facing half a dozen human problems, not only in our national life but in our international life, any one or two or three of which could tear the foundations out from under our entire civilization. We have the opportunity, if we are willing, to tackle the problem, putting up that sword, relinquishing our confidence, faith, or hope in any human administrations or human plans or agreements and... asking ourselves, 'Do I have the courage to take advantage of this opportunity to come out from under the law and live by Grace? Do I have the courage to declare within myself that I must no longer have faith in "man, whose breath is in his nostrils"? I must no longer have faith in princes, potentates, or powers, but actually retire within myself for an assurance of an inner grace.'"

Joel S. Goldsmith, "The Way,"
The 1960 Chicago Open Class.

❖ 11 ❖

THE INFINITE WAY OF LIFE

THE INFINITE WAY is a way of life to which we are led at some time in our experience. It is a way that cannot be told to any person: he has to seek it; he has to want it. Since all of us are at different states and stages of consciousness, not one of us can be ready for every message at every moment. So it is that there is always a moment in your life or mine when we are ready for this particular way of life.

The purpose of The Infinite Way is to bring about a transition in consciousness from a material sense of life to a spiritual consciousness of life. In this work a transition is made out of the world of material and mental powers to a state of consciousness where there is no power. Spiritual power is really not a power in the sense of doing anything to anything or anyone, or being used for any purpose whatsoever.

Assume Control over Your Mind

In the material sense of life, matter and material power in its many forms, down to and even beyond the atom, can be used. As we advance, we come to a place in consciousness where we can use mental powers and can control what goes into our mind or what comes out of our mind if we so desire.

Most persons are not only at the mercy of material powers and forces, however, but unfortunately they have not learned how to control what goes into the mind and what goes out from it. When they find one of the metaphysical movements,

189

they learn that they have jurisdiction over the mind. They can choose not only to read spiritual or metaphysical literature, but they can also choose to refuse to entertain the fear-thoughts of this world. By accepting their dominion they can refuse admittance to anything undesirable.

It is you, individually, who must, at some time or other, refuse any longer to be a victim of universal beliefs, of the malpractice of the world or the domination of the minds of men, refuse to be taken in by false advertising or by the millions of unseen and unheard thoughts that travel through the air. In other words, you must assume responsibility for your own mind, both as to what goes into it and what comes out from it. In this way you determine the nature of your entire experience because you learn how to avoid accepting universal beliefs and how to avoid the pitfall of coming under the domination of the thinking of others, individually or collectively. Thus, you can learn how to go through life in control of your own experience.

Refuse to Accept Negative Beliefs

Many students, in their first study, believe that there is some kind of mysterious power they call God that will take hold of them and do things for them that heretofore they have not been able to accomplish. It takes a while to realize that there is no such outside force, not even for good. The only force or power there is, is that which you yourself possess. You have within yourself the Redeemer, the Savior, the Power unto your own existence. So in your early experience, you learn how to choose, and thereby how to refuse entry into your consciousness of the negative beliefs, theories, and doctrines of the world. To some extent, at least, you become master of your own fate.

At first it may appear that you are using one power with which to overcome another power. It is not that at all. If I have believed that two times two is five and then learn that two times two is four, I have not used any power to change the five into four. I have merely learned the untruth of five and the truth of four, and in that process have not used any power whatsoever. In the same way, once you learn that God, or Spirit, constitutes the reality of being, that all power is in God, you learn also that what the world calls evil in any form—sin, disease, false appetite, germs, weather, or climate—is not power. These have been power only because of your acceptance of a universal belief in two powers.

Becoming Free of Erroneous Beliefs

Suppose that you have a cold and you are going to ask for a spiritual healing of this cold. The practitioner to whom you turn has no power over colds and neither has God. Nobody has power over a cold any more than you have power over two times two is five. You know that two times two is five is incorrect because you know that two times two is four. You have not used any power: you simply have known the truth, and by knowing the truth you have become free of an erroneous assumption.

The practitioner never heals a cold. He merely knows the truth that since God never made a cold, it has no spiritual power, no spiritual presence, no spiritual law; therefore, it has no existence in the kingdom of God. It exists only as a universally accepted belief in two powers. The cold should be very quickly met, not because the practitioner has any power over it, but because the practitioner knows the truth that spiritual substance, spiritual life, and spiritual law are all that really exist, and any belief in a cold is as suppositional and as erroneous as a belief that two times two is five.

You do not use the power of truth over error. You become free of the erroneous belief that there is such a thing as a cold in the kingdom of God. Once you know this truth, the kingdom of God has come on earth as it is in heaven.

If you follow the teachings of The Infinite Way, you will never seek the power of God or the power of truth to do anything to error. You will know the truth, and the appearance, which we will call five, dissolves because now four has been revealed, truth has been revealed.

A Life of One Power Has To Be Lived

If you were to begin this moment to live such a way of life, think of the changes that would have to take place in you to arrive at this state of consciousness. How many things do you know of now that you would like God to do something about? Think of how many things there are in your life or in the lives of those close to you that you would like changed by a God-power or a God-presence. Then remember that from this moment on you have given up that way of life and substituted for it the way of life in which you recognize no power in any negative or evil appearance. Whether that negative or evil appearance is appearing to you in the form of sin, false appetite, disease, lack, limitation, unemployment or whatever it is, let your attitude be:

Now I am living a life in which I recognize the nonpower of whatever it is that heretofore I have feared, whatever it is that I have felt required healing, changing, improving, or reforming. I no longer need a power to change, alter, improve, or heal anything.

Do you understand why this is a way of life? Just by declaring this, you cannot remove all the errors of your experience: you have to live with it and apply it until your whole consciousness changes. Remember that over the centuries you have built up a consciousness of two powers in which you have always been looking for some great power to do something to evil powers. This is the basis of orthodox theology, trying to get God to stop wars, to destroy our enemies, or to heal our diseases. And all down through the centuries it never has happened.

Accepting God as Omnipotence
Demands a New Way of Life

To remove the discords, inharmonies, and inequalities of life does not entail finding a God that you can pray to: it entails knowing the truth. The truth always is "Resist not evil."[1] To the paralyzed man, the truth is, "Arise, take up thy bed, and go unto thine house,"[2] or to the man with the withered hand, "Stretch forth thine hand."[3] There is never an appeal to God, not even in the presence of death. Death is not a reality. God has no pleasure in your dying. God is life eternal. God is omnipotent.

When you accept God as omnipotence you have adopted a new way of life, because now, under no circumstances, would you ever do any praying for the removal of evil. Your whole way of life would be realizing within yourself, "Omnipotence means all power; therefore, there can be no power to this appearance, not any more than there can be power in the appearance of the sky that sits on the ocean or on the mountain or, as Marconi discovered, no power in the air to prevent the passage of the messages that are to be sent." Accepting God as omnipotence makes for a new way of life.

Omniscience Changes
Your Way of Praying

What happens when you accept God as omniscience? Omniscience means all-knowledge, all-wisdom, all-intelligence, all-knowing. Watch how you enter a new way of life when you accept the truth of omniscience. How will you pray when you know that God already knows? What do you think you are going to tell God? What would you like to tell Him in your prayer? Would you like to tell Him that you are praying for Mrs. Jones? Are you going to tell God Mrs. Jones has rheumatism? No, the right to tell God anything has now been taken away from you.

Try to think what your prayer would be if you were called upon to pray for yourself or anyone else and were faced with the truth that God is the all-knowing, the infinite wisdom, the all-intelligence. Is there anything left to tell God? So your prayer would be a settling down somewhat like this: "There is no use in my speaking to the Father. The Father knows. My whole inner attitude is changed because now I have no message for God. I have nothing to tell divine Intelligence. I sit here in the realization that the Father already knows what things I came here to pray for. All I can do is sit here until somehow, some way, something within me stirs and tells me that the prayer is answered, the prayer that I never had to speak or think, the prayer that I never had to voice or write.

This is a way of life. You have to train yourself to be able to sit in quietness and in confidence and receive divine Grace without asking for It, in the full confidence of the Master's words: "Your heavenly Father knoweth."[4] Your whole function is to be still. In quietness and in confidence you will receive your answer.

If God is omnipotent and omniscient, all-power and all-wisdom, what chance would anyone have to influence God to do something that God is not at this second doing? Do you think that by taking thought you could make God do something that God is not now doing? Do you think you could move God out of Its orbit and hold back the sunlight for five minutes for some reason or other, or have the sun set five minutes sooner or later? Could you influence God to heal somebody? Do you believe that if God had any aware-ness of disease He would not do the healing before you spoke to Him? Be assured, since God is the all-knowing, God is not waiting for someone to tell Him that Mrs. Jones needs to be healed of rheumatism.

The Healing Agency Is
Omnipresence Consciously Realized

This is a new way of life, not really new, but practically so, discovered just four or five thousand years ago, and we are just getting around to re-discovering it.

As you read Infinite Way writings, you will notice that we approach this particular way of life through a knowing of the truth, a great deal of it. We do not use the letter of truth for the purpose of healing anybody but merely to elevate our-selves to a state of consciousness above the mental.

The healing agency in this way of life is God's presence consciously realized. If there is any secret to the message of The Infinite Way, that is it. The Infinite Way began with the discovery that in spite of omnipresence, God is not available to you or to me until God is consciously realized. For hun-dreds of year, even though people have been singing beauti-ful words in their hymns about omnipresence, they were not really believing a word of them. Here and now, in this way of life, you have to believe in omnipotence, omnipresence, and omniscience, and you have to act as if you believed.

Importance of the Listening Ear

Now here where you are, God is. The kingdom of God is within you. The Father has promised that all that He has is yours. Then what is wrong if you are not experiencing it? You have not been still enough to accept it. So you learn to have one or a dozen periods a day of stillness in which you recognize that since God is already the all-knowing, you are not going to try to tell God anything, and since God is omnipotent, you are not going to try to influence God. Since God is love, you are going to be still and know that *I* in the midst of you is God and that *I* will never leave you. *I* will go before you to make all things right. Then be still. Be still, if it is only for thirty seconds.

In the beginning of this way of life, if you do not seem to have any response within yourself, do not be discouraged because even though you may have no inner feeling about it or receive any inner message, your listening ear is the assurance that your prayer will be answered.

The Spiritually Endowed Become Servers of Mankind

There are periods in our study when coming together lifts everyone in the group to a higher state of consciousness. "I, if I be lifted up from the earth, will draw all men unto me.[5]... Where two or three are gathered together in my name, there am I in the midst of them."[6] You are attracted to a group because you expect that the word of truth will be spoken, a message given with other truth-students gathered together.

Your motive is to be in the presence of God, in the temple of God, which means the consciousness of God.

If, however, after one, two, or twenty-two sessions, you feel like being alone in meditation for a day or a longer period, or just going out once in a while to unite with others on this same path, that is the way for you to follow. You must be led by the Spirit that is within you. There are some persons who will find it very beneficial to make themselves a part of a group for a long, long time, until their consciousness has sufficiently developed so that they can stand alone for longer periods. There are others who have already come to a point where they can be more and more by themselves, and come out only occasionally to unite with some group that is definitely high in consciousness. Follow what will deepen and enrich your own consciousness.

This is a choice you have for awhile. There comes a time when you will not have this choice, because if you seriously follow a spiritual way of life, eventually you will find yourself spiritually endowed. When the Master spoke in the Hebrew temple, he said, "The Spirit of the Lord is upon me, because he hath anointed me to preach the gospel to the poor; he hath sent me to heal the brokenhearted, to preach deliverance to the captives, and recovering of sight to the blind, to set at liberty them that are bruised."[7] From the moment that he was ordained, he was not the master of his own life. He was a servant of God and a server of mankind.

Ordination Demands
Obedience to Inner Orders

If you follow a spiritual path far enough, you will find that at first you have a choice as to how to follow it and to what extent, but eventually the Spirit will take over and tell you how many hours a day you need of study or meditation. It will tell you whether to unite with others and share your life with them or to receive the light that they are shedding.

Eventually, when your particular spiritual work is given to you to do, you will have no choice as to whether it interferes with your home life or your social life. At the moment of your ordination you will be under orders. You have no control over this any more than you have control over God. You have no control over whether you are going to stay inside your present church or whether you will ever be a part of any church, for at a certain point in your life, the Spirit will take over, and It will give you your work to do. It may be inside some church organization or religious movement or it may not. That is the business of the Spirit. You have entered upon a way of life which is not your way of life, but God's way of life through you.

Then you will understand what the Master meant when he said, "Nevertheless not my will, but thine, be done."[8] Students make that remark sometimes, too, but be assured they do not usually mean it. Then can never mean it until that day of ordination comes when they really understand that to move contrary to God's will is as destructive to them as it was to Judas or to the young couple, Ananias and Sapphira, who dropped dead when they tried to violate their contract with the Christ.

Where human will is very strong, some are quickly thrown aside if they do not conform to the leading of the Spirit within them. While you have a choice as to where and when you will meditate, study, and read, exercise that choice in accord with what is revealing itself to you from within, but when the finger of God touches you and points a way, follow it.

Up to a certain extent, every person chooses his way of life. In the last analysis, however, you have no choice when the spirit of God has touched you. Once the spirit of God has set you on a spiritual path, It will not let you turn back, even though there are rare exceptions such as Lot's wife. She left the old city, the old state of consciousness, and then probably heard some bee-bop music and looked back to listen to it. That was her finish. You cannot look back to the city, to the consciousness you have outgrown, even when it was a pleasant one.

Sing Your Way Through Life with Is

This way of life is the way of no power. If you adopt the spiritual way of life, you have to sing your way through life in the realization of the word *is*. God *is*. Do you doubt that? Then where is God? God is omnipresent, everywhere present. Then God is where I am. What is God? God is omnipotent, the all-power and the only power, and God is omniscient, the all-knowing, all-intelligence, all-wisdom. But you can shorten all that into the two words: God *is*.

If you see some form of sin, disease, death, lack, or limitation, what must your instantaneous response be? God is! In this statement you have said, "God is present right where the discord seems to be; God is the power right where the discord seems to be; God is all the knowledge and wisdom necessary right where the discord seems to be." You can release the entire situation into the truth that God *is*.

What have you done in that realization? You have known the truth which is completely contrary to the appearance. The appearance testifies to sin, disease, death, lack, or limitation. This is two times two is five, staring you right in the face in great big letters, surrounded with electric lights, and probably in color to make it more alarming. In the face of this appearance, you have to say with Paul, "None of these things move me."[9] You have to be able to stand still in the *is-ness* of God.

This is a way of life. You have to change whatever way you have been living, such as running off to a corner and sitting down to hold your head and giving a good treatment, or thinking, "Well, now, as soon as I get home, I will give that a very fine treatment," or "Oh, if I could only contact God!" That is a way of life that is now denied you. You are permitted only one way of life that knows, "Here where I am, God is." Since God is no respecter of persons, that applies to everyone, even in far-off China and Russia. Why is God not effective in so many places? Because God is not recognized as omnipresence, omnipotence, omniscience.

No One Is Outside God's Grace

If you do not know this truth of *is-ness*, and if you flounder around mentally or prayerfully trying to get into God's grace, you will fail. You have to accept the truth that God is just as much God to a sinner as to a saint. You must give up the old theological superstition that there are people outside of God's grace. No one is outside of God's grace. All that is required to bring yourself into the manifestation of God's grace is to lift up your eyes.

Regardless of your sins of omission or commission, never believe for a moment that God's grace is any further away from you than it is from the saint. To be consistent in this, be sure that wherever you behold a sinner, you are also recognizing that omnipresence is there, just as the Master in his day was there to say, "Neither do I condemn thee."[10] There is no judgment.

As you proceed through life, a tremendous change has to take place within you as you learn to refrain from reaching out for a God-power. You have to refrain from any such reaching out because of the word *is*, or the word *am*. God is; I am. In that statement there is no such thing as "I will be" or "I might be after a certain number of treatments or prayers." You must have a total change of consciousness to where you can declare, in spite of all appearances, "Thank You, Father, I already *am*."

That is difficult, because you may be facing Pharaoh's army in back of you and the Red Sea in front of you. You may be facing a whole multitude to be fed. You may be facing three temptations in the wilderness, or you may be facing Gethsemane. In spite of all appearances, you have to abide in *is* and *am*. God *is*, therefore I *am*, for I and the Father are one. It is God's *is-ness* that constitutes my *am-ness*.

ACROSS THE DESK

The life of every Infinite Way student should sing the song of thanksgiving daily and hourly, not merely on one day of the year. The real thanksgiving that rings in our hearts has no earthly trappings of blessing-counting. How limited a concept of this deeply spiritual activity it would be to look at the apparent abundance of our human life and stop there with our gratitude! No, our thanksgiving reaches the kingdom of heaven itself and rejoices, not in the loaves and fishes, but in the consciousness of the activity of God as our individual being and as the being of all those with whom we have contact.

Thanksgiving is a spiritual experience that springs from inner wells of joy. It is the acknowledged fulfillment of spiritual consciousness that rejoices in its own beauty and bounty. We are grateful for the abundance of supply, harmony of relationships, and health of body, but we do not let ourselves stop at that level. We sing our song of thanksgiving out of the heart and soul of our Christ-identity which is our assurance of infinity.

TAPE RECORDED EXCERPTS
Prepared by the Editor

Years ago, long before the many classes Joel gave from1953 on, he said that there would never be another Infinite Way class unless it revealed a higher concept of prayer. Then came *The 1953 Los Angeles Practitioners' Class*, followed by class upon class on prayer. Hardly a class was ever given in which there was not great emphasis on how to pray aright because prayer reveals what is. Below are excerpts from some of these classes pointing out the importance of prayer in the spiritual unfoldment of an individual.

Prayer Can Change Your Life

"Prayer is an atmosphere. It is an atmosphere of consciousness, an atmosphere of thought, an atmosphere of the soul, and we must dwell in that atmosphere. ... Paul called it praying without ceasing; but to say, 'Pray without ceasing,' may impart to us, through our false sense of prayer, the idea that we must be continuously talking to God, asking of God, or affirming. Our sense of praying without ceasing will not be that. Our prayer without ceasing will be the living in an atmosphere of prayer, living in the continuous realization of God's presence as an unfolding Presence, as well as an unfolding life of joy and peace.

"Our world of effect represents our translation or interpretation of the divine universe. In other words, this that is before us is the kingdom of God, this that is named earth. It is only earth while we see it as limitation, while we see it as personal activity. The moment we see this universe through the atmosphere of prayer, we behold it as it really is and we are satisfied with that likeness. We behold this universe through prayer as the temple of God in which nothing ever has entered that 'defileth... or maketh a lie. ...'

"There is only one way in which we can rise above the evidence of the senses, one way in which we can rise above the appearance of sin, disease, lack, age, death. That way is through prayer, but not the prayer of asking God to give or withhold, not the prayer that has its basis in the belief that God is withholding something and we are now turning to God for an outpouring of that which up to this moment He or It is withholding. Is that clear?

"Our first approach to God in prayer must never be for God to give or for God to stop withholding, but rather, our prayer must be the realization of the continuous unfoldment of all that God is, and then bring ourselves into the atmosphere that releases that realization in our consciousness. ... This is the only moment we have in which to begin; this is the only place in which we have to begin; and it is here and now that we will begin our prayer. That prayer will be a relaxed sense in which our first thought will be gratitude... that God is and that God is love.

"We will drop every desire that we have ever sent in the direction of God. We will withdraw all forms of the prayer of expectancy of something from God. We will rest in the atmosphere of fulfillment."

Joel S. Goldsmith, "Atmosphere of Prayer,"
The 1953 Los Angeles Practitioners' Class.

"Close your eyes and realize, 'I'm seeking the grace of God; I'm seeking some word that proceedeth out of the mouth of God. I know not what to pray for, so I'm not going to pray for anything of this world.' ... Already a minute has gone by, but that minute has emptied you of your human thought about prayer. And so, for the next half minute at least, you have nothing to say. That's all; that's all there is to that period of meditation.

"That alone, repeated a dozen times a day, would change one's entire life inside of a month, or at least it would begin to show a change inside of a month, because every time one turns inwardly that way, he would be declaring, 'I can of mine own self do nothing,' even if he did not think the statement. He would be declaring, 'I'm seeking the kingdom within,' even if he never thought of those words. His whole attitude would be, 'Father, I can of mine own self do nothing. Come to my rescue.'

"It would be humility; it would be acknowledging the nothingness of human wisdom, human power, human strength. It would be acknowledging that there must come something from the Infinite Invisible. Something must come forth from the depths within us if we are to be saved, and all of that is the true sense of humility and the true sense of prayer. Those periods of silence create an atmosphere. Every blanking out of ourselves is making room for our Self, and this creates an atmosphere of Spirit, an activity of Spirit that, without our knowing it or having any awareness of it, goes before us to make the crooked places straight."

Joel S. Goldsmith, "How to Pray,"
The 1955 First Kailua Study Group.

"Every time we begin any work, we make it an occasion for prayer, but... no words and no thoughts enter into our prayer. Our prayer is a uniting of ourselves with God. What good would words do? What good would thoughts do if we were in violation of that which is necessary to establish contact or union with God? We now come to the higher sense of prayer in which we have recognized that taking thought will not add one cubit to our stature. ... And so we are through with words and thoughts, and have entered that place of communion, of conscious union with God, actual contact or the experience of God. ...

"Loosing all erroneous concepts, acknowledge the presence and the perfection of God—the Is. Then stand in that consciousness of oneness and let the light shine within. Now prayer is an activity of the Soul, ... an act of Grace, not an act of man. Prayer is an act of God taking place within me; it is a union with God, a contact with the source of infinite good, and it is done without words and without thought. It is done by standing still in being, with no judgment, no criticism, no condemnation, no praise, no flattery, not even praise of God. ...

"Prayer in it highest sense is the prayer of contact, of communion, in which no words or thoughts pass form you to God, and there may not even be words or thoughts passing from God to you, but there will be an awareness; there will be an inner sense of communion, an inner sense of peace. True prayer comes to its completeness and its perfection when there are no desires in the mind. True prayer, which is communion, comes to full bloom when one has lost all sense of wanting something in this feeling of communion, resting in the Soul. It is just as if all your wishes had been granted, ... as if it were Christmas morning at the tree. You had received all your gifts and now just have the feeling of 'Thank you, everyone.'

"When our consciousness is lifted to that sense of 'Thank You, Father; thank you, everyone,' then comes the fullness and completeness of communion with God, and in that there is a resting in the Soul. As a little babe rests in its mother's arms, so does that resting come to us in the Soul. But the babe has no desires; it has no wants, no needs: it is at rest. So do we come to a period of refreshment and a rest in proportion as we no longer take thought for what we shall eat or drink. ... We rest, never seeking—not even mentally desiring—but, rather, sitting back in pure rest.

"At every period of the day we are the beholder. We do not strive for supply: we behold supply as it unfolds to us from infinite sources. ... We never pray for health: we become still; we rest in the Soul. We let this prayer of the Soul take place while we nestle in Its warmth and watch as health or opportunities appear. ...

"We sit in perfect stillness until we feel that 'click,' feel that contact, that overpowering sense of joy or warmth, of gratitude, of love, and in that love we take in the entire universe. In that love, we take in friend and foe, without words, without declaring it, without saying it but by *being* love, feeling love, feeling a love that passes understanding because it is not a love of person."

> Joel S. Goldsmith, "A Meditation,"
> *The First 1953 New York Closed Class.*

"The Father within... is an infinite intelligence and... a divine love. ... When you know those two things about God, never again can you pray to God for anything; never again can you acquaint God with something that you believe you need. ... You have an entirely new concept of God that forever destroys your old sense of prayer. Your old prayer has to go. You have nothing to stand on, no way to tell God, who is infinite Intelligence, no way to ask God, who is already divine Love, whose good pleasure it is to give you the kingdom.

"If you were to learn only those two things about God, it would change your entire approach to life. Never again would you ask, seek, or knock for anything, but you would ask, seek, and knock morning, noon, and night for God's grace, for God's understanding, for God-awareness, for the God-experience. Your entire thought would be addressed to yourself to open yourself to the omnipresence, which God is, and the omnipotence and the omniscience. ...

"Through knowing the nature of God, you begin to know the nature of prayer. And you say, ... 'What becomes of my prayers to God? Either I must stop praying, or I must find a new idea of prayer.'

"As you do this daily, your affairs begin to improve. You can't see it immediately. It is only about a year later, when you look back and say, 'What, all that has happened to me this year! And I wasn't noticing it!' or 'Have I changed that much?' or 'What happened to those headaches I used to have?' or 'Where are those corns I used to have?' All of a sudden you notice that these... are gone."

Joel S. Goldsmith, "The Christ, Prayer, Inner Communion,"
The Second 1956 Chicago Closed Class.

THE TRANSITION TO CHRISTHOOD

IF YOU EVER seriously undertake to "pray without ceasing"[1]—to pray with no desire, no expectancy, and no wish to get or receive anything—you may immediately begin to think of all the different things you have believed God could give you. Once you begin to live the spiritual life, you will see what a tearing apart of yourself it is. It is exceedingly difficult to take the attitude:

God, I do not want anything; I do not need anything; I am not coming to You for anything. I am releasing You. You have no responsibility for me whatsoever. There is nothing that I need; there is no thing You have that I want.

The I-Am-ness of Being

There is a statement in the textbook *The Infinite Way* which reads: "That which I am seeking, I am." That one sentence could change your entire life, and it would, if it were understood and if you developed the capacity to live it, so that if at any moment a thought came to mind of "I need," "I want," "I desire," or "I wish I had," or your thought reached out to God for anything, this sentence would come back to you: "That which I am seeking, I am." What does that do to your sense of prayer? What are you seeking? Truth? "I am the way, the truth, and the life."[2] Are you seeking supply? "I am the bread of life."[3] Are you seeking health? "I shall yet praise him, who is the health of my countenance, and my

God."⁴ Now you cannot desire anything; you cannot want anything; you cannot even go to God for anything. You have to abide in this truth, "That which I am seeking, I am. ... I am the way, the truth, and the life.²... Neither shall they say, Lo here! or Lo there! for, behold, the kingdom of God is within you."⁵

The Son Lives in the I-Have-ness of Being

If you are abiding in the truth that "I and my Father are one,"⁶ you are under Grace because you are living by such promises as "Son, thou art ever with me, and all that I have is thine."⁷ Take that scriptural promise: "All that I have is thine." I! It all comes back to I: all that I have. I, the Father, and I, the son, are one according to scripture, and according to all revealed mystical truth, "I and my Father are one." What do I, the Father, have that I, the son, do not have, if I, the Father, and I, the son, are one?

The point now is to live in the constant remembrance that all the Father has is yours, for I, the Father, and I, the son, are one. That keeps you from reaching out to God, and it breaks all attachment to the world. It also keeps you from reaching out to "man, whose breath is in his nostrils."⁸ You no longer expect justice, love, benevolence, or anything else from man. You know now that all that you receive you are to receive from the Father, and yet not receive, because all that is embodied in the Father is embodied in the son. Prayer has to be the constant recognition, "Thank You, Father, I am"— not "I need," not "I want," not "I shall be," not "I should be," or even "I deserve to be," but I am.

Breaking the Prison Bars

Think of a prisoner in prison saying, "I am free." Yet, since he and his Father are one and all that the Father has is his, that has to be the attitude. The freedom of the Christ is the freedom of his individual being. In spite of all appearances, to experience that freedom he has to live and move in that consciousness.

Now, instead of prison, let us suppose you are imprisoned in a false appetite, a sin, or a disease. In spite of the appearance, there is no use praying to God to release you from your disease because God is not going to do it for you any more than for all the people on sickbeds at home or in a hospital. There has to be a different truth from that of praying to God for something, and this is that truth:

The spiritual freedom of the Father is the spiritual freedom of the son. "Where the Spirit of the Lord is, there is liberty,"[9] but since I, the Father, and I, the son, are one, then the Spirit of the Lord is where I am. Here where I am, God is. The place whereon I stand is holy ground because I and the Father are one.

As you abide in this truth, the prison bars—whether they are iron bars, disease bars, or sin bars—begin to break. Sometimes miracles happen in a flash, but sometimes it takes days, weeks, months—even years—to dissolve the particular fetters that bind you. There must be a constant living, moving, and having your being in the truth: *I* am the truth—not that there is a truth that will free you, not that there is a God that will heal you, but that you are one with the Father and all that the Father has is yours.

Why then are you praying for anything when you have omniscience within you, the All-knowing? Why are you praying for anything if you have omnipotence within you, the All-power? Why are you praying to God when you have omnipresence within you? God is no further from you than your own breathing, and since God is the All-knowing, you do not have to pray to God for anything: what you do have to do is to abide in the truth of your oneness with God.

Your Consciousness Determines Your Experience

Nothing enters your experience except through your consciousness. There is no God outside of you; there is no devil outside of you; and there are no laws outside of you. Whatever is operating in you is operating through and in your own consciousness, and it is one of two things. It is either a consciousness of truth or an ignorance of truth.

If you are ignorant of truth, you are not free but, if you know the truth, the truth will make you free. It is the knowing or the consciousness of truth that makes free. You must consciously know the truth—not sit around waiting for some mysterious God to do something for you because you are charitable, kind, or moral. It will not work. It is your abiding in the truth, your abiding in God and letting God abide in you. You are the one who must do it.

Let Truth Dissolve the Appearance

You probably are familiar with that metaphysical cliche about preying on God? The moment you stop p-r-e-y-i-n-g, the moment you are no longer the parasite seeking to draw something from God and live in the realization, "'That which I am seeking I am.' *I*, the Father, and I, the son, are one," you will have discovered the secret of answered prayer. By consciously knowing the truth you are abiding in the consciousness of truth. You are abiding in the Word, and the Word is abiding in you. You have to hold to that while ignoring the appearance that would testify to your present lack and limitation. If you are faced with lack and limitation at the moment, do not deny them because they may be all too apparent, but you can begin to ignore them as you abide in the truth and let the truth dissolve and dissipate them.

A Recognition of Your Relationship to God Reveals Infinite Supply

To live under Grace means to give up a great many universal human beliefs. There was a time when it was believed that because a person was in spiritual work, God would see that he had ample supply, and then, when the supply was not there, he found that God did not much care whether he was in spiritual work or not.

As a matter of fact, to God there is no such thing as spiritual work. There is no one needing supply; therefore, it is not God's function to supply. You must move out from the belief that because you were born, God owes you a living; or because you are a good wife or a good husband, a good housewife, a good mother, a good employee, or a good employer, you deserve supply. This is all in the realm of fiction. Nobody deserves supply, but everyone who recognizes and realizes his relationship to God is assured of infinite supply eternally flowing from the spiritual Source.

Humanly, there are thousands of ways of getting money, property, and securities. Spiritually, there is only one way. It is not by earning or deserving it; it is not by being worthy of it; it is not by giving God ten percent so that you get back ninety percent. It is not sacrificing to God; it is not spending so many hours a day in prayer to God.

There is only one way to enjoy the infinite abundance of God, and that is through knowing the truth. The truth you have to know is your relationship to God. *I*, the Father, and I, the son, are one, and the Father is always saying, "Son... all that I have is thine." As long as you keep looking to *I*, you will be abundantly supplied.

Let Your Expectancy Be From God

Human beings have been taught for centuries that a husband owes his wife support, and it is comforting to a wife to know and believe that her husband owes it to her. If you are a wife, what does it take to release your husband from the obligation to support you? What kind of an attained state of consciousness—*and it must be an attained state of consciousness, not merely the desire to appear spiritual*—do you think it really takes inside yourself to say, "I free you; I loose you; I accept from you whatever out of love you give, and I accept that as the love of God. But I release you from human or legal responsibility, because I am accepting my divine relationship to God, and I am declaring that 'I and my Father are one,' and my Father has infinite ways of bringing unto me that which is my own." As a woman, this is not easy.

But do not think for a moment that it is easy for men either because they have something equally serious that is holding them in bondage. They believe that their supply is from their business, their profession, their inheritance, or their investments. Furthermore, in this modern day, what would the world do without its Social Security and old age pensions? What do you think it really takes for a man to go within and inwardly know, although not outwardly say, "I will continue to work and to love my work, but I release everyone from the strain of believing that my supply is dependent on anyone. I have a conscious relationship with my Source. I have my personal relationship with my Father, and I and the Father are one."

Think of a salesman inwardly releasing his customers and silently realizing, "I look not to you for my sales. I sell as part of my business, but thank God, you have no control over my supply. 'I and my Father are one,' and my supply is mine in relationship to my conscious awareness of this truth."

Do you see how you are bringing yourself out from under the law of human belief, human relationships, and human channels of supply, and bringing yourself under Grace? No one can permanently bring you under Grace but you, yourself. Every time a practitioner brings about a healing for you—physical, mental, moral, or financial—he has released you from whatever law was operating and has brought you under Grace.

Come Out From Under
the Law and Live Under Grace

To be healed spiritually, you must be released from living under the law. Under the law, contact with certain germs is supposed to result in a cold or some other kind of disease. When you turn to a person for spiritual healing, however, he has to remove you from the material sense of law and bring you under Grace to where that law of infection or contagion is no longer operating, or the law of food, or the law of climate.

It is not possible for anyone to separate you permanently from living under the law. That is something you do for yourself. Your practitioner does it for you in an acute condition for which you turn for help. If a practitioner could do it for you permanently and completely, however, he would be too busy to give you help. Those with unlimited resources would engage him on a continuing basis, and he would have no time left for you.

But spiritual healing is something that money will not buy. You cannot even hire a practitioner or teacher by the month or year, and certainly not for life. It will not work! *You* have to move out from being under the material sense of law to being under Grace. In any emergency, of course, a practitioner who knows the truth of spiritual identity and the nonpower of effect can bring you out from under the law and place you under Grace in a particular situation, and probably in the next one, the next one, and the next one. But after a few years it does not work that way any more. In other words, sooner or later the student must begin to bring himself out consciously from under the law and bring himself under Grace. He must at some time or other release himself from traditional prayers or new modern metaphysical prayers that seek to gain something from God.

Breaking the Fetters of Human Experience

Release God, and let Him go:

You owe me nothing, and I seek nothing from You, or of You. You have already imparted Yourself to me, and all that You have is mine.

You begin to live under divine Grace, and then you find that less and less are you under the law. Less and less are you under the laws of weather, climate, and food; less and less are you under the laws of infection and contagion; less and less are you under the law of age and calendars; and more and more do you move into a life by Grace. It is a gradual process.

It is true that when you come to a transitional point, something happens, and in the twinkling of an eye you are completely under Grace. In other words, at a certain period of your experience, the fetters fall away; the law falls away; the past falls away; and you are under Grace. Actually you have brought yourself there through the years of seeking God, seeking truth, seeking realization. Because of your years of study and meditation, gradually you slough off traits of humanhood and thus prepare yourself for a certain moment when you are free.

In one blinding flash, Saul of Tarsus was free. He realized the Christ, and Saul was dead, and Paul alive. So now Paul could say, "I can do all things through Christ which strengtheneth me.[10]... I live; yet not I, but Christ liveth in me."[11]

That is what happens on the spiritual path. Day by day the transition is made; some fetter of human experience is broken, and some phase of humanness is dropped. Your prayer now is a benediction to the world and to you. You no longer pray that you receive anything, but rather:

Father, forgive my enemies: they know not what they do. Father, forgive those who despitefully use me: they know not what they do. Father, forgive all those who are not in Thy grace and bring them under Thy grace.

You have made an about face, and you are no longer sitting at the feet of the Master. You are now the Master, healing and freeing the multitudes, feeding and forgiving the multitudes.

Be the Master-Consciousness

As Christ-consciousness, you now seek nothing for yourself. Now you know that all that the Father has is already yours, and your whole life is pouring forth God's grace to this world—but not in the form of throwing your "pearls before swine"[12] to be trampled upon. You do it silently and secretly.

Your praying is done in secret. The "Father which seeth in secret shall reward thee openly."[13] Therefore, you do not go around blessing your fellow man so that he can see you do it or even know that you are doing it. It has to be a secret within yourself, known only to yourself and to the Father within. Then, as someone on the outer plane is led to you and asks questions or seeks, you can begin to share with him. If you are wise, you will do it as the Master did, by giving "milk"[14] to the babes in truth and meat to the adults. You will begin to pour the truth, the milk of the Word, out gently until you see that those who have come to you are ready for more truth. Ultimately you pour it all out; ultimately you give it all to them.

The life of prayer is not a life that goes to God to receive blessings. It is a life which fits you to be a blessing, so that you come out from sitting at the feet of the master and you, yourself, become the master who walks up and down the earth silently, secretly saying, "Neither do I judge thee. Neither do I condemn thee. Thy sins be forgiven thee. Thou art the temple of God, and God is in His holy temple. The peace of God is with you; the presence of God is with you; the omniscience of God is with you. 'The place whereon thou standest is holy ground.'"[15]

Now you are the master; you are the Christ-consciousness. No longer are you a selfhood apart from God, seeking, needing, desiring. Now you are the way, the life, and the truth, and you can be that only as long as you keep it secret. You can be that only as long as you keep this relationship between you and your Father secret, until somebody evolves to the extent where you can reveal this to him.

Gain the Consciousness, and the Rest Follows

Prayer is a way of life lived by the Master, the way of life lived as Christ-consciousness. That has always been your goal. You have always prayed that you might be given Christ-consciousness, that you might receive the Christ. The only way you can really pray for the world is by realizing, "I and the Father are one, and all of God's grace that flows to me will flow out from me, through me, to this world."

You cannot pray that peace come on earth. And why not? If peace came to earth tomorrow, there would be a war the day after. There would have to be, because man's consciousness has not changed. How can you have peace on earth while there is war in consciousness? Do you not see that all peace treaties would be of no avail unless the men and women of the world were ready for peace?

It is much the same with prosperity. People pray for prosperity, and then after they get it, do they not waste it? Think of all that is thrown away. People have had it; but they do not know enough to hold onto it. So there is no use in praying for prosperity until there is a consciousness of what to do with prosperity once it is attained. Gain the consciousness first, and then the rest will be added.

Accept the Truth of Christhood

You have prayed for the Christ to enter your Soul. As a matter of fact, *The World Is New*[16] is based on a quotation in the chapel at Stanford University, selected by Mrs. Stanford herself: "The world is new to every soul when Christ has entered into it." But are you going to sit around forever waiting for the Christ to enter in? It will not happen; it will not happen! Human consciousness has been prepared all these years to receive the Christ and to accept the truth that "I and the Christ are one." Now is the time to accept that truth; now is the time to move from being a person who surrenders even the right to pray in that sense, and understand:

Now, consciously, I and the Father are one, and all that the Father has is mine. My life now is one of bestowal, one of benediction, one of sharing.

You are standing looking out, not as a suppliant at the feet of the Master, but sitting at the left and at the right of the Master, co-workers with the Master, disciples of the Master, apostles of the Master, engaged in the one activity of sharing God's grace with humanity. So you pray: "Thy sins be forgiven thee. Father, open their eyes."

War or Conflict Cannot Enter Your Life if It Is Ruled out of Consciousness

Peace will come into your life when you individually are ready for it and not before. When you stop taking up the sword of criticism, judgment, condemnation, and malpractice, the sword will not be taken up against you. When you decide to live under Grace, under love, judging no man, that is the moment when peace will come into your experience, and no matter how many bombs are dropped, no matter how many thousands fall at your left or at your right, destruction will not come near your dwelling place, and you will be the means of saving many others who are a part of your consciousness. Peace will come to you when peace is established within you and you establish peace with your fellow man.

Prosperity will come to you when you are fit to receive spiritual prosperity by giving your first fruits to God, by giving of your conscious awareness to mankind. When you become the master, the disciple, or the apostle who is the instrument through which God's grace flows to mankind, peace and prosperity will be revealed as your experience. You will hasten the day when it will come to mankind, because mankind is still going to hold to its arrogant nature until there are enough Christ-apostles and disciples walking the earth forgiving and praying for the enemies of mankind to soften their hardness and apparent unreceptivity.

If the army, navy, and air force of every country in the world were scrapped, do not believe that this would bring an era of peace on earth. It would not. I have twice witnessed navies scrapped; I have several times seen peace treaties signed. Unfortunately, these things mean nothing. They are scraps of paper, because behind those pieces of paper there is no intention of keeping the agreements. In other words, there is not yet the mellowness of love in human consciousness.

But once that mellowness comes into human consciousness, treaties will not be needed any more than the United States needs a treaty with Canada. The United States has no peace treaty with Canada, nor does it have any armies and navies at the Canadian border. And why not? Because on that side of the border and on this side of the border there has entered the consciousness of peace. Yes, there will be problems between Canada and the United States for a while. Always in human relationship there come disturbing elements. This is not war, however, and it cannot eventuate in

war because peace is already established in the consciousness
of these two nations of North America.

So it is that you will discover that war or conflict cannot
enter your life if it has been ruled out of your consciousness. But it cannot be ruled out of your consciousness while
you are living on the human plane, which is under the law.
It can be ruled out of your consciousness only if you will
accept yourself as the Christ, or as a disciple or apostle of
the Christ, and realize that you have moved from the human
state of consciousness to the spiritual. You are now at that
place where your life is a life of forgiveness, a benediction, a
blessing, and no evil can come nigh you because you are not
seeking anything. You are not even seeking good. As long as
you are not seeking, you are not going to receive. You will
always *be*. This is your real nature: *being!*

*I and the Father are one in being and in essence. I and the
Father are being life; we are being eternal life. I am immortal
life.*

Move Up Beside the Master

When do you move from that seat at the feet of the
Master where you beg, "Give me life," to that seat beside
the Master where you acknowledge, "You have given me life
eternal. I am life eternal"? When do you move from asking
to be fed to saying, "You have fed me with truth, and now
I know that all that God is, I am; all that the Father has is
mine"? Make the transition in consciousness. Move up to
that place beside the Master. You can bring this about if you
will begin this very moment to realize that the privilege of
going to God or to man for anything has been taken away
from you. Even in the midst of a prison, a prison of sin or of
disease, you must close your eyes to the appearance, beg no
more, plead no more, but realize:

Thank You, Father; all that You are I am. "That which I am seeking, I am." All that You have is mine. Here where I am is holy ground, for here the spirit of the Lord is, and "where the spirit of the Lord is, there is liberty."

The letters this year have charted that movement or transition in consciousness from sitting at the feet of the Master to sitting beside the Master with the realization, "I have received from the Master. I have received life eternal; I have received divine Grace; I have received the assurance of my oneness with God. Now it is my turn to share, to bless, to pray."

Praying for the World

In praying for the world, there is one mode and means of prayer that will do more to break the evils of the human mind than anything else:

God, Spirit, is omnipotent, and therefore, the mind of man is not power, the will of man is not power, the way of man is not power. All power is in God, Spirit, and therefore there is no power in the carnal mind, mortal mind, or the human mind.

Christ is not a temporal power that goes out and destroys enemies; Christ is not a temporal power that goes out and kills your enemy. Christ is not a power that goes out and helps you strike a better bargain at someone else's expense. Christ is the gentle presence that establishes peace in the heart, mind, and soul of men. Look upon the Christ as the gentle influence that cements men in their spiritual relationship. Do not look upon God or the Christ as a temporal power that you can invoke to go out and do something, but understand that the carnal mind of man is not power, and the gentle influence of the Christ is the dissolving of all that is adamant in human consciousness.

To pray for the world means to look out as if seeing this globe of the universe in front of you, and feel your hands or your love going out around that globe with "Father, forgive them, they know not what they do. I pray that your sins be forgiven you. I pray that the Christ dwell in your heart. I pray that no penalties ever be inflicted upon you for the past. I pray that you know spiritual freedom, spiritual justice, spiritual life, and spiritual law."

Hold that globe in a whole armful of love, understanding, and forgiveness, and allow no thought of victory to enter your mind: no victory over man, no victory over ideologies, no victory over nations—not victories, but peace. There never can be peace when there are victories, because with every victory there is a loss, and the loser must always think about the next possibility of gain. Never think of victories: think of peace. "My peace I give unto you."[17] Keep that globe in your arms: "'My peace I give unto you: not as the world giveth, give I unto you,'[17] My peace, spiritual peace, the peace that brings with it forgiveness and comfort. My comfort give I unto you; spiritual comfort."

Remember that you have moved. You are not sitting at the feet of the Master; you are sitting beside the Master, and you now have the right as a disciple or an apostle to place your arms around the globe and say, "'My peace I give unto you: not as the world giveth.[18] ... My grace is sufficient for thee'[18]—not charity, not benevolence, not somebody's generous pocketbook. 'My grace is sufficient for thee.'" You are speaking out as a disciple of the Master.

The most difficult situation arises with yourself in the early months when you have to resist consciously the temptation to want or desire something, as if you were out there as a suppliant at the feet of the Master. Consciously you have to remember that you gave up that seat to those who are not yet aware. Now you are sitting as a co-worker with the Christ of God. Your function is no longer to receive, but to bestow. Your function is not to get, but to give. The question that you must ask yourself every morning is, "What have I in the house?" Then throughout the day, as the opportunity comes to bestow the bread of life, the meat, the wine, the water, the life, the resurrection, remember that that is the path upon which you have embarked.

Each day you must remember what you have in the house from the standpoint of a disciple. You will find you are living your life in a different dimension, and certainly you will find that you are living under Grace, because now, like the disciples, you can go out without purse or scrip.

Are you still under the law, or are you under Grace? That depends on where you are sitting. It depends on whether you are looking out at people, remembering what they owe you and seeing to it that you get it, or whether you have come to realize your relationship with God and can understand yourself to be the bestower, the giver, the sharer of His glory. You are not giving anything of yourself. You will not be one penny poorer after you give away a thousand, because it is not yours that you are giving. That, too, determines whether you are under the law or under Grace.

Do you believe that your personal possessions are yours, or do you see that "the earth is the Lord's, and the fullness thereof,"[19] and God is just expressing Itself through you? That makes of you a transfer agent. You are not a giver of your own; you are not a giver of yourself: you are merely a transfer agent. "The earth is the Lord's, and the fullness thereof," and "Son… all that I have is thine." Keep your eyes on that word *I;* "All that I have is thine." You and the Father being one, you have allness to give, to share, and to bestow. So it is that through the letters this year you have moved from one who is seeking to one who *is*.

ACROSS THE DESK

Much has been written on the spiritual significance of Christmas. The words, moving and inspirational as they are, however, are without meaning if the student has not embraced the deep spiritual significance of Christmas in his own life as a daily conscious experience.

Christmas signifies the emergence of Christ-consciousness into the world to dissolve world hypnotism, thereby healing the sick, supplying those in want, and binding up those sick at heart. To The Infinite Way student, Christmas is a daily experience. Through meditation and daily prayer work for the world on the part of Infinite Way students, spiritual consciousness flows out as light dispelling darkness.

Without this daily experience of Christ-consciousness, Christmas has little real meaning. In the daily activity of meditation for the world, however, we are paying homage to the Christ-child within, a greater homage by far than the kings and wise men of old brought to the child Jesus.

ABOUT THE SERIES

Readers often ask, "How can books by Joel Goldsmith have been published after his transition in 1964?" For many years, Joel worked with his editor, Lorraine Sinkler, to publish a monthly letter for students who wished to subscribe to it. The annual collections of these letters were later published in book form. After Joel's transition in 1964, Joel's wife, Emma A. Goldsmith, requested that Lorraine continue to publish the monthly letters by drawing on the vast library of tape recordings of Joel's class work. Again, the collections of annual letters became books.

Acropolis Books is privileged to have published the 1971 through 1981 Letters as a series of eleven fine-quality soft cover books. Like all of Joel Goldsmith's other books, these are now available as e-books. To review the entire library of Goldsmith print and e-books, visit www.acropolisbooks.com.

SCRIPTURAL REFERENCES AND NOTES

1. PEELING OFF THE ONION SKINS

1. Matthew 23:9
2. Luke 15:31
3. Matthew 24:44
4. Exodus 3:14
5. John 8:58

2. GOD MUST BE AN EXPERIENCE, NOT A CONCEPT

1. Matthew 4:19, 20
2. John 18:36
3. John 14:27
4. Isaiah 55:11
5. Isaiah 55:8
6. Hebrews 4:12
7. Job 19:26
8. Psalm 46:10
9. John 10:30
10. I Kings 19:12
11. John 14:9
12. By the author, *Living Between Two Worlds.* (Acropolis Books, Atlanta, 1996)

3. THE NATURE OF SPIRITUAL DISCERNMENT

1. John 18:36
2. John 7:24
3. Matthew 19:17
4. John 14:9
5. Matthew 16:13,15
6. John 8:11
7. I Samuel 3:9
8. John 10:30
9. Matthew 16:16
10. Matthew 16:17
11. Matthew 17:1-8
12. Philippians 4:7
13. Matthew 4:19
14. Philippians 2:5
15. Matthew 23:27
16. Luke 2:49
17. John 5:17

4. IMMORTALITY UNVEILED

1. Matthew 7:16
2. I Corinthians 13:12
3. Psalm 90:10
4. Matthew 19:17
5. I Kings 19:12
6. Matthew 3:17
7. Luke 15:31
8. John 18:36
9. John 4:32
10. Isaiah 45:2
11. I John 4:4
12. John 14:10
13. Isaiah 2:22
14. John 10:30
15. Matthew 24:44
16. Psalm 17:15
17. II Corinthians 5:1
18. II Kings 2:10
19. Matthew 16:16
20. Matthew 16:17
21. Luke 23:34

5. CONTEMPLATIVE MEDITATION AND HEALING WORK

1. John 7:24
2. Matthew 19:16,17
3. John 5:30,31
4. John 7:16
5. Hebrews 10:8
6. Matthew 16:17
7. Matthew 10:34
8. By the author, *Living Between Two Worlds*. (Acropolis Books, Atlanta, 1996)

6. THE MIDDLE PATH

1. Isaiah 1:18
2. John 18:36
3. Luke 12:14
4. Exodus 20:3
5. John 5:30
6. Hebrews 4:12
7. Isaiah 55:11
8. Mark 5:34

7. Is

1. By the author, *The Infinite Way.* (DeVorss & Company. 2002)

2. John 2:19

3. Luke 4:13

4. Matthew 26:39

5. I Corinthians 13:12

6. Psalm 23:1

8. MIND IMBUED WITH TRUTH

1. Romans 8:17

2. I Corinthians 3:16

3. John 18:36

4. John 16:33

5. Psalm 17:15

9. THE CHRIST KINGDOM

1. Matthew 26:52

2. Isaiah 2:22

3. Isaiah 61:1

4. Philippians 4:13

5. Romans 8:11

6. II Corinthians 12:9

7. Job 23:14

8. Psalm 138:8

9. John 10:30

10. Luke 15:31

11. Psalm 23:4

12. John 9:25

13. John 14:27

10. REJECTING APPEARANCES AND CONCEPTS

1. John 14:2

2. John 18:36

3. John 4:32

4. John 6:35

5. By the author.

6. Matthew 5:20

7. Matthew 11:11

8. Acts 17:24

9. By the author. (Acropolis Books, Atlanta, 1999)

10. By the author. (New York: Harper and Row, 1963)

11. Hebrews 13:5

12. Matthew 28:20

13. John 6:35

14. John 11:25

15. Matthew 23:9

16. Psalm 46:10

17. John 2:32

11. THE INFINITE WAY OF LIFE

1. Matthew 5:39
2. Matthew 9:6
3. Matthew 12:13
4. Matthew 6:32
5. John 12:32
6. Matthew 18:20
7. Luke 4:18
8. Luke 22:42
9. Acts 20:24
10. John 8:11

12. THE TRANSITION TO CHRISTHOOD

1. Thessalonians 5:17
2. John 14:6
3. John 6:35
4. Psalm 42:11
5. Luke 17:21
6. John 10:30
7. Luke 15:31
8. Isaiah 2:22
9. II Corinthians 3:17
10. Philippians 4:13
11. Galatians 2:20
12. Matthew 7:6
13. Matthew 6:6
14. Hebrews 5:12
15. Exodus 3:5
16. By the author. (Acropolis Books, Atlanta, 1997)
17. John 14:27
18. II Corinthians 12:9
19. Psalm 24:1

Joel Goldsmith Recorded Classes Corresponding to the Chapters of This Book

Many of Joel Goldsmith's books, including this one, are based on his recorded classwork, which has been preserved in tape, CD, and MP3 formats by The Infinite Way Office in Moreno Valley, CA.

The listing below shows the classes related to each chapter of this book. For example, "#159-1 1956 Chicago Closed Class 2:1" means:

The recording number is 159, Side 1 (**#159-1**).

The recording is from the **1956 Chicago Closed Class**.

The recording is Tape 2, Side 1 for the 1956 Chicago Closed Class (**2:1**).

1. Peeling Off the Onion Skins

#710-1: 1955 Chicago Reading Room First Anniversary 1:1
#710-2: 1955 Chicago Reading Room First Anniversary 1:2
Excerpt: #523-2: 1963 Kailua Private Class 8:2
Excerpt: #143-2: 1956 First Steinway Hall Practitioner Class 4:2

2. God Must Be an Experience, Not a Concept

#45-1: 1953 First New York Practitioner Class 1:1
#103-1: 1954 Seattle Closed Class 1:1
Excerpt: #183-1: 1957 Chicago Open Class 1:1

3. The Nature of Spiritual Discernment

#540-1: 1964 Honolulu Infinite Way Study Center 4:1
Excerpt: #440-2: 1961 Hawaiian Village Open Class 4:2

4. Immortality Unveiled

#486-2: 1962 Los Angeles Special Class 1:2
#49-1: 1953 First New York Closed Class 2:1

5. Judge Not According to the Appearance

#46-1: 1953 First New York Practitioner Class 2:1
#46-2: 1953 First New York Practitioner Class 2:2
#74-1: 1954 Honolulu Lecture Series 10:1
Excerpt: #61-2: 1954 Chicago Practitioner Class 3:2
Excerpt: #16-2: 1952 Honolulu Closed Class 3:2
Excerpt: #89-2: 1954 New York Practitioner Class 1:2

6. The Middle Path

#46-1: 1953 First New York Practitioner Class 2:1
#46-2: 1953 First New York Practitioner Class 2:2
Excerpt: #27-2: 1953 Los Angeles Practitioner Class 1:2

7. Is

#47-2: 1953 First New York Practitioner Class 3:2
#74-1: 1954 Honolulu Lecture Series 10:1
Excerpt: #117-2: 1955 Kailua Study Group 8:2
Excerpt: #158-2: 1956 Chicago Closed Class 1:2

8. Mind Imbued with Truth

#483-2: 1962 Princess Kaiulani Closed Class 4:2
#222-2: 1958 New York Closed Class 4:2
Excerpt: #27-2: 1953 Los Angeles Practitioner Class 1:2

9. The Christ Kingdom

#433-2: 1961 Canadian Special Class 3:2
Excerpt: #16-1: 1952 Honolulu Closed Class 3:1
Excerpt: #89-2: 1954 New York Practitioner Class 1:2
Excerpt: #63-1: 1954 Chicago Closed Class 2:1

10. Rejecting Appearances and Concepts

#418-1: 1961 London Open Class 5:1
Excerpt: #234-1: 1958 London Advanced Class 3:1
Excerpt: #365-2: 1960 Hawaiian Village Open Class 3:2
Excerpt: #323-1: 1960 Chicago Open Class 3:1

11. The Infinite Way of Life

#465-1: 1962 Pacific Palisades Special Class 1:1
Excerpt: #29-1: 1953 Los Angeles Practitioner Class 3:1
Excerpt: #114-2: 1955 Kailua Study Group 5:2
Excerpt: #50-2: 1953 First New York Closed Class 3:2
Excerpt: #161-2: 1956 Chicago Closed Class 4:2

12. The Transition to Christhood

#466-2: 1962 Pacific Palisades Special Class 2:2

Made in the USA
Columbia, SC
14 March 2023

13743046R00139